MARRIAGE

and the

FAMILY

by

A. J. HIGGINS M.D.

Published by
GOSPEL TRACT PUBLICATIONS
411 Hillington Road, Glasgow G52 4BL

ISBN 0 948417 29 3

First Printing, May 1988
Second Printing, May 1991

Printed by
GOSPEL TRACT PUBLICATIONS
411 Hillington Road, Glasgow G52 4BL

To my wife, Ruth, without whose patience, love and understanding the lessons and the writing of this book would have been impossible.

Contents

Foreword

"Marriage and the Family" was published as the lead article for thirteen months in the *Truth and Tidings* magazine. They were longer than normal magazine articles with the intention that they would be published as a book. During the time they were running in the magazine, hundreds of requests were received and are still being received that these articles should be given a more permanent form. In our ten years with the magazine, we have never seen such a response to anything we have published. The present book is the result.

The value of the material will speak for itself. Dr. A. J. Higgins is a practicing physician who, in his clinical practice, is daily answering questions that relate to home and family. He has excellent training and has gained a wealth of experience, but the truth taught in this volume is from Scripture. We have been deeply impressed that throughout this entire subject, Dr. Higgins has not resorted to a psychological approach with a few Scriptures added on to give it a Christian flavor. The truth taught is the exposition of Scripture, with practical application that is in full harmony with the interpretation of the Word of God. It is our conviction that these chapters will have a far wider circulation than the readership of *Truth and Tidings* magazine. Mr. Samuel F. Johnston of Gospel Tract Publications, Glasgow, Scotland is handling the printing and binding as well as the distribution of this book.

We want to take this opportunity to express our deep indebtedness to our dear friend and brother, "Sandy" Higgins, for the many sacrifices of time and effort that he has devoted to the work of the Lord. We also owe a great debt of thanks to his wife, Ruth, and their two daughters for so freely sharing their husband and father's time for the blessing of so many others.

We highly recommend this teaching as being an excellent guide for a Christian couple contemplating marriage. It is also a most valuable guide to young parents as they face the solemn responsibilities of raising a family at the close of the 20th century. We even recommend it to those who have been married for many years as a refresher course in what it means to truly care for one another, that their lives may be fuller and richer and lived more for the glory of God and the blessing of others. There is a chapter that deals with an unmarried believer, this has already proved to be a blessing to many.

As these pages are sent out, they are accompanied by our prayers that God will richly bless the effort that has gone into their writing to the enriching of many lives. "Let the word of Christ dwell in you richly in all wisdom" (Col. 3:16-17)!

March 1988 Norman Crawford

CHAPTER ONE

Building the Basis

When George Washington was appointed commander-in-chief of the Continental forces at the outbreak of the Revolution, he replied to the Congress by saying, "Although I am truly sensible of the high honor done me at this appointment, yet I feel great distress from a consciousness that my abilities and experience may not be equal to this extensive and important trust...I beg it be remembered by every gentleman in the room that I this day declare with most sincerity, I do not think myself equal to the command I am honored with." The feelings of the writer run in a somewhat parallel course with his illustrious predecessor.

The idea of contributing a series of articles on marriage and the family is a bold undertaking for anyone. For someone with a family still being raised, and not even a silver anniversary in his past, this may seem dangerous. When it was suggested that I consider contributing this series, I was not enthusiastic.

Yet the need exists and we cannot ignore it. The reader will, however, not find this a "how-to" manual on raising children and establishing the perfect marriage. There will be no insightful first person stories from the life of a victorious Christian and his family.

These articles will contain simply the scriptural

pattern and principles which should govern every family relationship. These are God's standards. If there is some flaw in the writer, it is not the standard but the saint who is at fault. Some might think that these are the musings of an idealist, someone divorced from the real world. Be assured that God's ideals are far above anything an idealist can imagine. If any should challenge us as to whether we have experienced in full the blessings of these scriptural principles, I would simply ask, "Who has ever exhausted all the joy and blessing from what New Testament Christianity has introduced?" In every sphere of our lives we can, like Paul in his relentless pursuit of Philippians 3, seek to press on.

In the first article of this series, we will look together at courtship. Not only is courtship the first event in time when considering the courtship-marriage-family cycle, but it also is the very basis for much that follows.

The Problem Defined

Some might think that an article on courtship will be an exercise in creative writing. What can one possibly find in the Scriptures concerning courtship? Eastern marriages were arranged with businesslike precision. Surprisingly, there are both principles and examples that will be of great profit for us to consider.

If anyone is not aware of some of the problems confronting our young believers in the area of courtship, allow me to articulate some of their concerns. One of the greatest fears of youth is failure and embarrassment. All of us can recall with a very uneasy feeling the emotional trauma that attended some of our early mistakes as teenagers and young adults. Unfortunately, the assemblies would qualify as a subculture with its own rapid communication network. News spreads from Boston to Toronto to Vancouver to Washington and back with amazing speed and accuracy. All of this has its advantages to us but it also has its liability to young people. A rejection of a person by another soon becomes common knowledge; a break up in a relationship carries with it the added spiritual toll of a public failure. For how could one have "known" the Lord's will about their relationship and then have it end?

Perhaps we, as older believers, should be more careful in our spreading of news, more reserved in our "gossip." It would doubtless at least spare a lot of feelings and embarrassment.

How are young people to get acquainted? How are they to know the character of others without keeping company? Any interest soon becomes interpreted by others in a more serious light than usually intended. Talking together soon means that the couple are soon to be married. The overly sensitive avoid suggestion of interest for fear of gaining, unjustly, a reputation for lightness. Others court this reputation flagrantly. These are very real problems which our young people face. Answers are not always as easy to formulate as questions. Not everyone will be satisfied with what follows, but read on.

Coupled with this is a very relevant question, Is marriage for all? The Lord Jesus spoke of those who cannot marry and others who chose not to marry for the Kingdom of God's sake. More on this in a later article.

The Priority Discovered

I was recently asked an excellent question: "If marriage is really the second most important decision a person must make in their life, why has God allowed it to be so subjective?" We have all been at crisis decision points in our lives and have wished for a book of rules, some plain guidelines for decision making.

Recently, there has appeared in evangelical circles a new teaching. Its main theme is that there is no such thing as a specific will of God for your life. Simply stay within the broad scriptural guidelines and whatever you do is fine. Translated into everyday terms, this new teaching states that since the Scriptures only require you to marry a believer in the Lord, any believer who fits this description will do. Don't worry yourself over a particular one that the Lord has for you.

This might sound like a tremendous burden lifter for those of you who are spending hours, days, weeks, even years waiting upon God for an answer to a specific request. Though it has the appearance of a great spiritual tranquilizer, it is, in reality, a robber of spiritual blessing. Waiting upon God serves many purposes. Many believers gladly testify that the experience of seeking God's mind is often as valuable as the expression of God's mind. The refining process, the wait which is so difficult for the flesh, frequently brings our priorities into focus. This is perhaps a partial answer to the question that headed this section. God has made the matter subjective that we might be cast more upon Him and learn our hearts and develop priorities in this most important realm.

The Purpose Declared

What is the purpose of courtship? This might sound to the sophisticated as a relatively naive question. Allow the question to have its place on the page and its moment in your thoughts. Dating should never take character from the world. The purpose of courtship is with a view to marriage, the joining together of two to become one, a union intended to be of the total person for the total life. Dating for "fun" has no place in a believer's thinking. Emotions are too vulnerable. It is for this reason that you should begin praying as early as possible that God will keep you from error and direct you to the right person. To only begin praying when your emotions are involved is to wait too late. Our hearts are deceitful enough without the added bias of infatuation. Even in situations where friendship is the avowed intention of the two, one is usually hurt in the end. Every courtship then should be with a view to determining if the person is God's choice as your partner in life.

The Pattern Discussed

Where then can we look for help in the Scriptures in attempting to find principles to guide us in this important step in life? Courtship and dating can't be found in Strong's or Young's Concordances.

The best place to begin a search is in the first three chapters of Genesis. If we search together here, we will not be disappointed. Notice carefully what is written in Genesis 2:22, "And the rib, which the Lord God had taken from man, made He a woman, and brought her unto Adam." Did you notice how the Spirit of God has expressed this primal courtship? God brought her to Adam. Amazing statement! One would have thought Adam of sufficient common sense, and Eve likewise so gifted as to realize that, with the absence of anyone else, they were meant for each other. Yet God did the bringing together. Is this lesson, stamped as it is on the very first pages of our Bibles, to be lost upon us? Hasn't God put it right here for our instruction in this essential step in life.

Allow me the boldness of this simple question: If you are now keeping company with someone, do you have the consciousness that it was God who brought you together? Or was it a certain amount of manoeuvring, flirting, or chasing that accomplished this? Was it the makeup or the mind of God?

There is nothing that will give stability to your marriage and confidence when praying for the salvation of children born to that marriage as the firm conviction that God brought you together. Tragic to have to confess failure in courtship later when the children are not saved and are drifting away from the gospel! This by no means suggests or even hints that if children are unsaved the parents made a mistake. Further still, it does not imply that if parents find that they were wrong in marrying that they cannot own it before God and cry to Him to save their children. What I am emphasizing is the great confidence to be able to approach God knowing that my marriage and its fruit have been in accord with His will.

But come a little further along in Genesis to the well known story of Isaac and Rebekah. I can hear someone object that there can scarcely be anything here on courtship. This was a long distance engagement, arranged by an intermediary. Isaac had not even seen her before the engagement. While some in our reading audience may applaud the virtues of this method, we have to own that its practice is foreign to our culture. What then can we learn?

How did the servant "know" the right woman for his master's son? There were express requirements laid down by Abraham as to family, country etc. Could we liken this to the general guidelines of the Word of God as to a Christian, and marriage in the Lord? But then the servant asked for an additional sign. He would know that it was the right woman if she offered to give water to his camels. Why this sign? Was this a simple whim? A stab in the dark for a really unusual sign? Consider the possibility that what he was looking for was the expression of not only outward beauty, but character. The girl who would agree to the monumental task of drawing water for the camels was one marked by hospitality, kindness, consideration and a willingness to work; not bad qualities to look for in a prospective wife. The moral of this lesson is that Rebekah became a wife by displaying character, not cunning; by inner beauty, not outward attractiveness.

One more illustration may suffice for now. The story of Ruth the Moabitess is familiar to all. Naomi, her mother-in-law, enouraged her to return to Moab so that she could find a husband there. The prospects for a husband were almost nonexistent in Israel for a Moabitess damsel. Now Ruth was not ignorant or misled; she was no starry eyed idealist who hoped against hope that somehow her mother-in-law was wrong. Counting the cost, she returned to Bethlehem.

Mark now the lessons which flow from the ancient, yet fresh love story. How did Boaz become acquainted with Ruth? The first contact and impression was through her labour in his field. In the company of other young people, he had the opportunity to observe her. Her industry was observed by others. Boaz could ask the counsel of the servant over the reapers concerning Ruth. It soon became common knowledge in the city that Ruth was a virtuous woman (Ruth 3:11). Could this be a partial answer to a query raised earlier in this article? Group activities among young people form the safest way for initial impressions to be made. Obviously it does not allow the opportunity for more than a superficial knowledge, but it is a beginning. Many a prospective spouse can be scratched from the list with just this casual observation.

Boaz also asked others about Ruth. Don't be afraid to approach older mature believers for their counsel. Just don't stack the deck in your favour by going only to friends of the one in whom you have an interest. In the multitude of counsellors is safety (Prov. 11:14).

The end of the story finds Ruth in Boaz's home. How did she get there? It was not through chasing Boaz or "high visibility" techniques. She simply was carrying out the will of God for her life and God brought her into his field, family and future. That should be a great encouragement for younger men and women. God is able to control the circumstances that bring young men and women together.

Ruth needed one more lesson. She had to learn patience. "Sit still my daughter," counselled Naomi. Waiting upon God and patience are difficult for us all. My flesh does not differ from yours. Waiting is painful to us both. Yet, in waiting, God's will is perfected.

It may sound overly simple and perhaps a bit old fashioned, but can't God be trusted for a partner in life? Do we have to aggressively seek one? God will never give you second best for life if you are trusting Him. It may not be the person upon whom your heart is set, but it will not be second best for your life.

When someone has expressed an interest, would it not be better to wait together in prayer for God to guide further and confirm the interest and exercise? Letter writing can reveal more about a person than simply their ability to spell. This can be an effective means to know the priorities in a person's life. It can help to show their interests and goals. Someone may say that this is the ideal but is not realistic in our society. God has called us to manifest christian principles at every level of our life. Going for a walk together, going to dinner and other means of becoming acquainted are excellent for couples who are exploring their interest in each other. Absolute honesty is imperative between both, lest one be led along unkindly. In your courtship you are building the basis for your future together. The principles which have permeated your relationship up to marriage will not likely differ drastically from those that will control your days after marriage.

It must be stressed that these are not the workable principles of a particular subculture. It is not that we have to use this means because of our circumstances. These are divine principles that should be used because they will ensure the mind of God for you without the emotional cost of mistake and tragedy.

May I be allowed to address older believers for a moment in this article for younger Christians? If what has been written is true, how can we justify our frequent role as matchmakers. The writer is penning these words with embarrassment upon his face and a confession upon his lips. *Mia Culpa!* Yet if we are to be consistent with the idea that young people must discover the will of God for their partners in life, can we profess to know the mind of God for them? Can we dare risk pushing something if God is not in it?

Purity That Is Demanded

Paul could tell the Philippians that for him to pen certain things was not grievous to him and for them it was safe (Phil. 3:1). It may seem unnecessary to write of the demand for moral purity in your relationship, but suffer the reminder for the present. The examples of Scripture are abundant: Rebekah's veil, Ruth's behaviour, Joseph's initial concern over Mary's pregnancy; even Lot maintained moral standards for his daughters in wicked Sodom. They were virgins before marriage. The clear instructions of the New Testament should never be interpreted in the light of the Old Testament and its legislations concerning required marriages for premarital relationships (Deut. 22:28, 29).

These principles apply to both brethren and sisters. Since they are God given they apply equally well now as then. The standard, the ideal is high. As you strive to reach it, God will give what is best for you.

CHAPTER TWO

God's Pattern Under Pressure

The Patriarchal Pattern

A trip to your local evangelical bookstore should suffice to convince you that "marriage" is a big seller. Books abound on every aspect of marriage. You can learn how to select the perfect partner, begin your days together with "happily ever after" almost as a guarantee and, finally, rekindle your flagging relationship.

Current popular Christian writers have not discovered marriage, they have simply rediscovered what God long ago took great care to include in His exhaustive writings. You do have that volume. It is called The Bible.

Now some might feel that, while marriage is by no means something new, the many attacks and societal pressures on marriage today are indeed new and unique to our generation. A very cursory study in Genesis will quickly reveal quite the opposite. No sooner had wedding vows been exchanged in Eden's garden than Satan began working to disrupt, counterfeit and destroy marriage. He had very good reasons and relatively good results. Notice that Genesis 4 introduces Lamech with his wicked polygamy, the very antithesis of all that the union in the garden typified. Ham, in chapter 9, shows us indecency; adultery appears upon the scene in chapter 16; Sodom has become synonymous with homosexuality; incest shamefully makes its appearance in the royal family of Judah in chapter 38; prostitution in 38:24 and, finally, seduction, in chapter 39, complete the list. Not much has been added to the pressures and perversions of marriage by our twentieth century. Agreed that the restraints which once kept these sins at a minimum have disappeared, but the sins are the same though increased in acceptability by society, and in frequency.

Lest any of the readership should think that they are immune from satanic attack, allow the inspired words of Paul to reach your conscience and bring you into the presence of God for preservation, "That Satan tempt you not for your incontinency" (1 Cor. 7:5). If nothing else is impressed on us from this article, may we all be sobered to realize that Satan desires to mar and destroy everything in which God finds pleasure. That, solemnly, includes your marriage.

It is always rewarding to look in Genesis when seeking to find a God ordained pattern. This occasion is no exception. The marriages at which we will look together were not perfect marriages. They were marriages between imperfect human beings. Yet in these marriages, God was revealing something of His intention for what marriage should be.

Please accept these principles as they have been sent. They are not descending to you from the mountaintop of personal experience. They are sent in the spirit of one who is learning with you.

Adam and Eve — Leaving and Cleaving

God is a great teacher. He teaches slowly and patiently. He frequently teaches one lesson at a time. In Adam and Eve, the great lesson taught relates to oneness in marriage. God comes at this unity and impresses it on us from several different angles. If nothing else could impress this on us, certainly the words of Genesis 5:2 would suffice. He "called their name Adam, in the day when they were created." Two people with one name. As someone else has said, "In the arithmetic of heaven one plus one equals one."

Their unity is expressed first of all by the woman's unique origin. Other creatures were created from the dust of the earth (2:19). Here was a unique creature who came from Adam's side. She was completely different from all others from the very outset.

The importance of this one-of-a-kind creature was not lost upon Adam's intelligence. When Adam awoke from his divinely induced anesthesia, his first words were, "This is now bone of my bone and flesh of my flesh." God was instructing him in this oneness by the very origin of the woman.

But God sought also to teach us this oneness by the woman's unique suitability. Recall how that over all God's creation had rung out triumphantly the divine estimate that all was good. Strangely when God looked upon Adam He said, "It is not good..." What He was referring to was his loneliness. We are told that every creature was brought to Adam (2:9), but there was not found a help meet, or one who was suitable, for him. The idea of help is not a servant or assistant to Adam. The word will not allow such usage. Would it surprise you to find the exact same word used in Psalm 10:14 of God, "Thou art the helper of the fatherless," and again, in Psalm 22:19, "Haste Thee to help me," and again, in Psalm 30:10, "O Lord, Be Thou my Helper."

We must banish from our thinking any intrinsic idea of inferiority or servitude from the word help. The woman was to be a suitable companion for the man, his complement. There was, even before the fall, headship in Adam, under which the woman came, but that is not being stressed so much as their perfect suitability that enabled them to know the unity which God intended for them.

One final element appears to finalize the lesson which God is teaching from our primal parents. It is their unique relationship. If you think that perhaps God was not intending to teach as clearly as I am outlining, simply look at verse 24, "Therefore shall a man leave his father and his mother and shall cleave unto his wife; and they shall be one flesh." We have become so accustomed to reading these words that we lose sight of one startling fact: Adam had no mother or father to leave. Why has the Spirit of God inserted this here? He certainly wasn't instructing Adam or Eve. He is impressing on us God's great design and purpose for marriage.

"Leaving" is a strong word. It admits of no going back. This cannot be stressed too much. The ultimate purpose God has for oneness can never be known if there is not a "leaving." I recognize that this is addressed to the man. That does not excuse the woman. She moves from subjection to one headship, her father's home, to another, her husband's. It is the husband who has the great responsibility of establishing a new headship and forsaking his place of subjection in his father's house.

Leaving parents is not only a physical event. Would it be too practical to suggest that the word urges care in discussing your spouse's faults with your parents? Your loyalty is now primarily to your spouse. Ask for recipes or tips on home repair from your parents, but don't have counsels of war on how to change all your partner's bad habits.

"Cleaving" is equally strong in its implication and demands. When used in our New Testament it means nothing less than being glued together. Your lives are now one. It hardly needs to be said that this word allows no room for separation and return to parents when things are not going well. It is by bowing to the standard of Scripture that you will be forced to work out scriptural principles that will prosper your marriage.

The result of leaving and cleaving is that they become "one flesh." Since 1 Corinthians 6:16 describes union with an harlot as "one body," and not "one flesh," the union in marriage must be something more than just physical, although it embraces this. While it is not spiritual oneness, it is a unity that transcends simply the physical to involve the mental and emotional. I freely own that I do not as yet understand all that is involved in this oneness. I think, however, that we see in it the ultimate and greatest purpose of marriage. Some will contend that God instituted marriage, primarily, to populate the earth. If true, this would mean, that a childless couple is a failure; or that a couple which married late in life would never realize God's design. No such thing! When Paul writes in Ephesians 5:31-32, "This mystery is great," I firmly believe that he is speaking of the mystery of marriage. God had something hidden in His great heart and mind that was not revealed until He revealed it through Paul. The mystery that is great is not the church, it is the ultimate purpose of marriage.

Abraham and Sarah — Lordship

The marriage of Sarah and Abraham emphasizes lordship. This is not imagination, but the Spirit of God's commentary upon them. Allow me to show this. Recall how Genesis 18 chronicles Sarah's failure to believe God concerning the birth of a son. A low point indeed in her spiritual exercise before God had come. Have you ever noticed Peter's commentary on this in his writings? Read 1 Peter 3:6, "Even as Sarah obeyed Abraham calling him lord..." When did she call him lord? The only occasion which I can find is when she laughed and said, "After I am waxen old shall I have pleasure, my lord being old also." Notice this carefully and please don't miss the lesson which the Spirit of God has painstakingly provided. In a moment of failure God found something which He could commend about Sarah, she called Abraham her lord.

I hear someone objecting that she certainly did not act the part of a submissive wife in chapter 16, but a nagging, complaining wife. It well may be that this was because Abraham failed to act in his capacity as lord. But that does not change the fact that she did recognize him as such in chapter 18.

Submission is something foreign to our modern society. What must be understood by young couples is that submission is not a word that deals with essence or the quality or value of something, but it is an attitude word. Its usage in 1 Corinthians should settle that forever. God is given the place as the head of Christ, a concept which forbids any idea of inferiority.

Submission is not the road to getting your husband to do what you want; it is not a way to get him to change. The idea is not that if you play your role, then he must play his. Submission is commanded for its own sake and because it is a picture of the church's relationship to Christ (Eph. 5:22). Paul also mentions that it is to be as unto the Lord. This disallows any idea of bitterness or grudging submission. Paul admonishes in Titus that the older women teach the younger women submission "that the word of God be not blasphemed." In Colossians 3:18, the injunction is linked with Christ being all (everything) and in all (in every relationship). Finally it is Peter who suggests, in chapter 3, that indeed this is the way to be the greatest help and influence to your husband.

More will be said about what submission means in a future article. At this point we are simply pointing out that it was an essential ingredient of a

Genesis marriage, an ingredient which God commended.

Isaac and Rebekah — Love

We come now to a curious thing. If I, perhaps you also, had written Genesis, no doubt the scene in Eden would have included some reference to the deep love which Adam and Eve shared. If I had failed to place it there, I would certainly have included it in the touching story of Abraham and Sarah. Yet no mention is made of a husband and wife's love until we get to Isaac and Rebekah. Why? Were they the first to love? Or is God teaching us progressive lessons?

Could I intentionally overstate the truth at first, a truth that may sound shockingly strange to western ears and ways. Perhaps it is not that love is the basis for marriage, but rather that marriage is the basis for love. Now before you start writing your letters to the editor, please bear with me. Remember that I said I was purposely overstating the case.

But now notice the order in Genesis 24:67, "Isaac ... took Rebekah and she became his wife; and he loved her." Recall how Paul phrases it, "husbands (not fiancés) love your wives (not our intended)." The emphasis on love is always after the marriage. Please do not think that I am saying that love is not an important element in deciding upon marriage. The love, however, of the Scripture is not the sentimental soap opera emotion that hovers somewhere between lust and infatuation. It is not the theme which fills the lyrics of pop vocalists and poets. The more the world sings about this love and goes after it, the higher the divorce rate soars. Obviously this is not the cement which holds marriages together.

What holds marriages together is not love but a commitment, an unconditional, unbreakable commitment made before God to take each other as husband and wife. The implications here are critical. This means that couples cannot walk away from a marriage when they "discover that love is gone." This means that there is no excuse in "I can't love her anymore." Within the commitment of marriage love can flourish. It is only when I have the security that I am in an indissoluble relationship that I can allow myself to be known to my spouse. Without that security I cannot risk being understood. If I cannot take that risk I will never know the oneness of which Genesis 2 speaks.

If a couple should tragically discover that they should never have married, that they don't have the love for each other which they thought they had, what are they to do? God has commanded the husband to love his wife. If God has commanded it, then it must be possible. Learn to love is the Scriptures' advice.

At times, I have to sign forms with couples who are nearing marriage. I have used this as an opportunity to explore their concepts of marriage. I am dumbfounded to hear time and again that since they are in love all will be well. Sadly I see many of these couples return in the throes of separation and divorce. The secular world in which they live has popularized the idea that love somehow enables couples to conquer problems. The truth is that marriage magnifies problems.

From Isaac and Rebekah, I learn that in marriage, God has prepared a soil in which love can grow to its fullest potential, but this is only possible when both people recognize the permanency of their commitment.

Jacob and Rachel — Leadership

Allow me to end with the example of Jacob and Rachel. Jacob, we are told, also loved his wife. This love became the basis for his leadership. It was not a demented distorted idea of supremacy but genuine love which caused him to lead her and his family.

From Genesis 30:25; 31:4-14, I learn that Jacob discussed his plans with his wife (wives sadly), and took the time to hear what she had to say. He did not drive callously. In 32:21-23, he looked to her protection and safety; in 35:1-4, he took the lead in spiritual matters.

Jacob's failures even in marriage could be listed. That is not our concern. I have tried to show how, in these patriarchal marriages, God is teaching a grand design for our lives; leaving and cleaving to become one, lordship, love and leadership are the basic ingredients of a scriptural marriage.

I cannot define marriage well. If I were to attempt to summarize what we have learned together in Genesis, it would be that marriage is an unconditional commitment of two people for their entire lives, a commitment which not only embraces each other, but is an assumption of scriptural roles for each.

CHAPTER THREE

Enlightenment from the Epistles

Medical education has traditionally stressed a pattern which will serve us well here. The first year of training is an intensive education in what is normal concerning the human body. This is undertaken before any disease or abnormality is ever mentioned. After a thorough grounding in the normal, the abnormal or the diseased becomes apparent and easily diagnosed.

It is imperative that we see what God's ideal for marriage is from His Word before we examine the pathologic. We cannot measure God by what we see in the world. The love starved and lust driven world has exchanged convenience for commitment, divorce for God's demand for life long unity, and serial monogamy for marriage.

We will have to look at the Word of God if we are to discern God's mind for your marriage and mine. The previous paper discussed principles as seen in Genesis. In this paper we shall look together at the epistles which furnish ample material for our enlightenment.

An Explanation of the Principles seen in Marriage

It is from the pens of Paul and Peter that we learn much of what God expects from wives and husbands in marriage. The Pauline passage, in

Ephesians 5, is well known, but widely misunderstood. Everyone knows that Paul exhorts wives to submit and husbands to love. But what do these familiar terms mean? Does one response depend upon the other? Where are the list of rights which each partner has?

Look first at the wives' **attitude.** It is not without design that the injunction for submission comes before anything is said about the husband's love. The wife is not to submit because her husband loves her, but because the Lord has commanded it. Her submission is "as unto the Lord."

Her submission is not servile bondage nor blind obedience. The truth of subjection as seen in 1 Corinthians 11:3 should long ago have put to rest any such mistake. It is a willing submission to the husband's headship and guidance. It never presupposes an inferiority in person or intelligence. We are told in Luke 2:51 that the Lord was "subject" to Mary and Joseph; the perfect One was willingly submissive to imperfect mortals.

Her **affection** is also detailed in Titus 2:4. She is to be a lover of her husband and her children. Some often point out that the wife is nowhere commanded to love her husband. Here, in Titus, she is to be taught to be a lover of her husband and children. It is true that this word is not the *agape* love, but rather the *phileo* love. This however is not an inferior love, but a love which shares and enjoys. The wife is not called upon to have selfless, self-sacrificial love for her husband. That is uniquely his role to her; she is called upon to have the love of companionship, of sharing together, and warmth. Her affections are to be reserved for her husband and family.

Paul also touches upon the sphere of **authority** which the woman has. In both Titus 2:5 and 1 Timothy 5:14, she is a home ruler. It is here that her talents and intelligence are put to greatest uses. The ordering of a christian home and the creation of a sanctuary from the world is by no means something that calls for inferior intelligence and talent. No woman in the business world faces a greater challenge than the christian woman in the home. No career oriented feminist is using her intelligence more maximally than the woman who is a home ruler, transferring the atmosphere of heaven to a home on earth.

But what of the husband? Paul commands the husband to love his wife. Under this embracive term, the Spirit of God gathers together several thoughts.

His love is to be a **selfless** love. The love enjoined upon the husband is the *agape* love. It is a love which does not demand anything in return but seeks the good of the other. It is the love of 1 Corinthians 13, a love that has as its standard and eternal example the love of Christ for His church. It is not a love that is active in order that the wife might be submissive. It is not even a love that goes out so that it might be easier for love to be returned. It is a love that seeks only the good of the other. *Agape* love is the love which overcomes all the problems and woundings of marriage. It is love which does not ask, "What am I getting from this relationship?" but, "What can I give to this relationship?"

It is dangerous and difficult to generalize. It may

however safely be stated that most of the problems in marriage come from the basic problem of selfishness. The selfless *agape* love is the antidote to this.

This love is also by definition a **sacrificial** love. "Christ...gave Himself for it." The demands of love are far higher than the world has any idea about. We all use the word far too loosely. It is a word of high demand and import. A husband is called upon to sacrifice himself for his wife. While some might rise to the challenge if death were the only demand, to sacrifice ourselves daily in the many smaller mundane issues of life is far harder. We may not be called upon to go to the stake for our wives, but at times we could go to the store without grumbling. It is not so much laying down our lives as laying down the newspaper when our wives are talking to us.

Sacrificial love will touch upon my time and interests. I will be willing to give up time for my wife. I will be willing to put my own interests second to meet her needs. Marriage is a commitment to these principles. The man who is not ready to live these principles is not ready for marriage and would be wiser to forbear. Marriage is not simply an adding on to my other interests, but a restructuring of all my interests with a new priority. Far too often we are prone to enter into marriage with the concept that it will serve my interests better. The true Biblical view of love is far different. This self sacrificial love expresses itself in Ephesians 5 most practically as a **supportive** love.

We all need appreciation. It is one of the most

basic needs of the human psyche. "Nourisheth and cherisheth" are the expressions which Paul uses. They mean among other things to build up, warm up, cheer up. Paul warns of harshness and a lack of appreciation in Colossians 3:19. Men gain a large measure of satisfaction from their employment. Raises, reviews, and promotions all are a way of being told that your work is being appreciated. Have you ever thought of telling your wife how much you appreciate all she does in the home? How well she is doing with the children? How successful she is as a "home-ruler"? Speaking as a husband I know that there is a danger of taking our wives for granted. There is the possibility of thinking that we are out doing the real work and that the care of the home is minor. I am not now referring solely to the cleaning and domestic responsibilities, but to the creation of a true oasis, the transformation of a house into a home.

Marriage must be built upon mutual respect, care, understanding and love. We as husbands must cultivate a deep appreciation for our wives. The philosophy that permeates society often permeates our minds as well. We begin to look upon home making as a minor role; we begin to think that the real thing is only happening out there on the front lines of the business world.

Consideration will make you a student of your wife and her needs. Have you ever thought what it must be like for a mother to spend eight hours a day with several preschool children all demanding her attention simultaneously? After cleaning up the second glass of spilled juice and entertaining them for several hours, she can be emotionally exhausted. If the children happen to be very young, with vocabularies limited to monosyllables and sentences of two words at best, she may even forget what the English language sounds like. For a husband to come home at dinner time and immediately disappear into the study with "work" is not considerate or kind. I realize that time is needed for personal study and preparation for meetings, but a balance is needed. Your wife needs you as much as the assembly does. The Scriptures call upon you to sacrifice yourself, not your wife, for the things of the Lord. I am writing this conscious of such Scriptures as Luke 18:28-30 and 14:26. Paul, in 1 Corinthians 7, makes clear that only mutually agreed upon sacrifices are what God intends. Usefulness for God will entail sacrifice, but be sure that it is first self sacrifice and then a sacrifice that your spouse has agreed upon.

Peter is at no loss for words on this subject either. In 1 Peter 3:7, his counsel to husbands can be summarized by companionship, consideration, and communion. The husband is to recognize a difference in the natural sphere — she is the weaker vessel, and an equality in the spiritual sphere — heirs together. To cultivate companionship is not easy, yet it is commanded by Peter. It involves a sharing together of time, interests, and inner thought life. Men by nature have a difficulty with sharing. We have a mind set that this is a weakness. In sharing, however, true companionship and dwelling together occurs.

The application of *agape* love by every husband

toward his wife is not simply a theoretical, mystical business with Paul and Peter but an intensely practical and observable matter that expresses itself in the everyday affairs of life.

An Examination of the Picture Seen in Marriage

The standard as outlined by Paul and Peter may seem almost unobtainable. Where is the husband to obtain the grace needed for this most unnatural love? Where is the wife to secure grace for her role in subjection to her husband? Enter Paul's lucid description in Ephesians 5. Now before looking at this, there are perhaps two things which must be understood. Some have the idea that God looked for an object lesson through which He could teach men something about Christ and the church. The truth is that God instituted marriage with this in mind. It was not an afterthought, a fortunate stumbling onto a good example. God designed marriage with this great truth in mind, that from marriage mankind would learn something of Christ and the church.

The other error that frequently is made is to think that marriage is a miniature of Christ and the church. If this were so, then everything that is true of the one would be true of the other. In point of fact, marriage is a picture or an expression of this greater truth.

The wife in her willing submission to her husband has the great privilege of portraying the role of the church to Christ. A body must yield to the guidance of its literal head if it is to function properly. So in the family setting, proper order can only be known if there is no tension between head and body. In Ephesians, it is underscored that Christ as Head is also Saviour of the body. This sense of preservation in the spiritual body is transferred over to the unity of marriage with the implication that the preservation of marriage is best assured when the wife is subject to her husband.

Husbands are enjoined to love their wives with the same kind of love which Christ displayed for His church. That love not only sacrificed for her, but also raised her to her highest possible potential. Christ gave Himself at Calvary to effect positional sanctification and cleansing. This looks forward to a day when He will present the church to Himself without spot or wrinkle. Christ's love was selfless in that He gave His all to bestow blessing and honour upon the object of His love. A husband's love for his wife will elevate her to the highest level of womanhood, beauty and usefulness for God. The principles of the Scriptures will not demean woman but elevate her.

Perhaps the working out of these principles in marriage is seen best in the life of Aquilla and Priscilla. In them and in their marriage then we have an

Example of the Potential in Marriage.

This couple is first introduced to us in Acts 18. The first obvious feature about them is their **unity.** They are always mentioned together. Their unity is nowhere better expressed than when Paul in writing to the Romans speaks of Priscilla and Aquilla (plural) "who...laid down their neck (singular)." There is a suggestion in Acts 18:1-4 of **authority and subjection.** Aquilla seems to have taken the lead in the enforced move from Rome to Corinth, and Priscilla followed her husband.

The order of the names is not without its lesson. Depending on the version consulted, the six mentions of this godly couple are evenly divided, in three instances Aquilla comes first, and in three Priscilla leads. In matters of guidance and teaching Aquilla's name is first. In hospitality in the home Priscilla's name is first.

The usefulness fo Aquilla was made possible by Priscilla. When Apollos needed to be guided into more truth, this couple opened their home and heart to him. In the sphere of the home they were able to instruct him in the way of God more perfectly. Much that is done for God is done in the home. A willing wife is essential for this. At the Judgment Seat it is certain that the usefulness and blessing of many a brother will be acknowledged to have been possible only because of a cooperative wife.

If we have traced their **ministry** in Acts, Romans, and 1 Corinthians, in 2 Timothy 4:19 we are impressed with their **loyalty.** This was expressed toward the apostle himself, but also toward each other. Years have passed since they first were introduced to us in Acts 18, yet they are still together not only in name but in spirit. It reminds us of God's intention that marriage be a life long commitment of two people to each other.

Exhortation to Purity in Marriage

Before closing this article, would you permit me to mention something on the physical intimacy in marriage? To omit any mention would be to be guilty in the opposite extreme of what has become prevalent today. Modern writers and thinkers accuse some of hiding mention of physical sexual relationships in the closet. To "balance" this, they have placed it out on the front lawn. We should seek to see the place that God has given it in the marriage bond and appreciate its value.

Since Paul's letters were intended for public reading in the gatherings of the saints, we shall seek with reverence and the dignity becoming to a public magazine to look together at some of the Scriptures which deal with this.

In Hebrews 13:4, we are reminded of the absolute **morality** of physical intimacy in marriage. The sanctity of marriage and the sin of immorality are seen in this brief statement from the pen of the Hebrew writer, as he details a regiving of the moral law from Mt. Zion (Heb. 12). Physical relationships within the marriage bond are not defiling or unclean in any way. It is not an added attraction, a compensation for life's other problems. It is an integral part of the marriage, an act which not only expresses the oneness of marriage, but reinforces and undergirds it. There should be no shame or sense of reserve between a couple, but there should be openness and communication that will allow each to enjoy the full potential of the physical act of intimacy.

In 1 Thessalonians 4:3-8, we are given the **mandate and the motives** for purity. It is not simply a good idea, but a divine command. It is the will of God. Morality is not something that God has enjoined to limit the pleasure of His creatures. It is not a prison wall that has barred men from the real world of enjoyment. It is rather a fence around something of such tremendous value and joy that He is seeking to protect it from intruders who would spoil and mar it.

Premarital sexual relationships practice the unity of marriage physically without the unity emotionally or legally. It is an expression of a commitment which has never occurred. God intended physical oneness to be known only after marriage.

In 1 Thessalonians 4, we are given at least six reasons for morality: it is the will of God; it is consistent with knowing God; the government of God upon immorality; the call of God; the indwelling Holy Spirit, and the wrong of defrauding a brother.

Perhaps the main section on marital relationships is found in 1 Corinthians 7. Here we learn of the **Mutuality** in marriage. There is to be a mutual **consideration** one of another. The pleasure and joy of the partner is the chief concern (v. 3). In contrast, modern sexual therapists stress looking out for self. There is stress upon mutual **cooperation.** No longer is my body my own (v. 4) exclusively. It is not a contradiction to the principle of headship here, but something far higher. In this most intimate of all relationships, I willingly give consideration to another and her claims upon me. Selfishness has no place in physical sexual relationships. The sexual games that people play are unscriptural. I am referring to couples who punish each other by the use or withholding of physical intimacy, or even its use to gain an end other than the pleasure of a spouse. There may be periods where, for agreed upon reasons, physical union is not possible, but this is only by mutual **consent** as seen in verse 5.

The intimacy of marriage is not a duty I render my spouse, but a pleasure I am privileged to give. It is not nonspiritual but holy, right and scriptural. It should never be a weapon or tool I employ for my ends. This is reinforced in verse 6 by a mutual **concern.** There is a vicious enemy who will exploit even this most sacred and private aspect of our lives if we allow him.

CHAPTER FOUR

First Things First

It is a remarkable and delightful thing to see what can be learned of God in small details, in obscure verses. Consider what a revelation there is of the care and concern of our Father in heaven when the Lord Jesus revealed that not one sparrow falls to the ground without the Father's knowledge. Someone has said that God attends the funeral of every sparrow.

In a similar manner, we can learn much about God's idea of marriage from just one verse. You will recall that David used one stone of five to slay the giant; the Lord used one book from the Pentateuch to silence Satan. In like manner we need only one verse from one book to silence and slay many strange ideas about marriage.

Notice Deut. 24:5, "When a man hath taken a new wife, he shall not go out to war, neither shall he be charged with any business; but he shall be free at home one year, and shall cheer up his wife which he hath taken." While this furnishes a lovely and touching foreview of the Lord seeing to the joy and happiness of His heavenly bride before He goes forth to make war and finish the Father's business which He came to do (Luke 2:49), our main attention is drawn to the principles of marriage which are contained herein.

The first and most obvious lesson which lies upon

the surface waiting for our consideration is

The Priority of Marriage

When all the humour which we find attached to this verse is gone, we are left with some sobering conclusions as to God's thoughts about marriage.

Israel was and still is a nation which depends upon its military for its well being. Any nation that spends over 50% of its total budget on defense is obviously placing national defense as a top priority. But in the mind of God, there is something of far more importance than national security. More important, of higher priority than defending Israel's borders, was strengthening and stabilizing the marriage bond.

What is the lesson God is teaching? Why is the marriage bond of such priority that the new husband had a year off from military duty? Perhaps God is teaching through this that the future of the nation was really more dependent on good marriages than on a good military machine. But there is more. Not only was he relieved of all military responsibility, but he was also not to be charged in any business. The idea of being charged with any business is somewhat different. It is not the idea of buying and selling, simple occupational matters; it usually referred, in our Old Testament, to "official business" for king or nation. Recall how David used this term in 1 Samuel 21:2. The business of a wife took priority over the business of a king of nation. It is not national security as much now as personal honor that is in view. Not only was the new husband to view his wife ahead of the nation, but also ahead of himself.

In this modern day of role reversals and two working spouses, it may well be necessary to emphasize that neither wife nor husband should put a career ahead of the good of the marriage. Sacrificing a spouse for the purpose of getting ahead, or even for the apparent noble purpose of being a good provider for the family, is not scriptural order.

Some might object that spiritual relationships are to have the priority over all others. This is obvious and clear, yet yielding to the spiritual priority teaches me that a spiritual man will look well to the state of his marriage. The same chapter of Colossians that stresses "Christ is all and in all" (3:11), instructs me that the practical expression of giving Christ priority in my life is to give my wife priority and to love her with a selfless, self-sacrificial love (v. 19).

Responsibility in Marriage

God is a realist. Poets may write of marriage made in heaven, but heaven is wise enough to know that marriages require a lot of work on earth. To the husband is given the responsibility to "cheer up" his wife. As if to stress the magnitude of the task, he is given an entire year to accomplish this. Some might add that for some wives, the time allotted to do the task is all too short.

What is meant by cheering up a wife? Why does she need it? Isn't marriage an end all? what every woman is searching for to fulfil her childhood fantasies of playing wife and mother? We are impressed again with the fact that God is a realist.

Perhaps some insight may be gained by looking at the word used in Deuteronomy 24:5, "the wife which he hath taken." The word for "taken" is one that is also translated elsewhere in our Old Testament as marry, seize, lay hold of, snatch away. While we all would like to fit "marry" into the context, there is still a sense in which she has been seized, laid hold of, snatched away from all that she once knew. Her security, sense of belonging, at times, even friendships have been disrupted. She may search in vain initially for some of the kinds of love that she knew and needed in her pre-marital state. "Kinds of love" brings us to much of the husband's responsibility.

Sadly the English language uses one word for love, obscuring many of the nuances which the Greek language preserves. There are at least four kinds of love which we as humans can experience. Now before we begin dissecting and dividing, it is essential that we recognize that one type of love is not inferior to another. We are so prone to distinguish, for the purpose of applying a moral value, one over against the other. This is not the case here. Each love has its place and each literally enhances the other in the marriage bond.

Eros — The Flame of Marriage

Some may immediately object that this is the lowest form of love, that which is merely instinctive, catering to "baser" desires. But is this really so? We must distinguish between infatuation and romance. The former is based upon fantasy and continually demands reinforcement of one type or another. It feeds upon novelty and daring. Romance cherishes the object. This level is where many couples begin a relationship. But the relationship that remains here without progressing in marriage is doomed to failure.

Granted that *eros* is not used in our New Testament. Is it however totally absent from our Bibles? We read the Song of Songs with an eye to its spiritual application. This is right and proper. Yet in its setting, it is an account of pure and passionate love between a bride and her bridegroom. We have too long allowed the debasing of romance by the modern world to influence our views. Passion can indeed be pure and free of sin. In the marriage bond it is what has been called the "thrill" factor, that which adds excitement to a marriage. Look at Proverbs 5:15-20 to see how Solomon counsels a young man to enjoy romantic love with the wife of his youth.

It is important to realize that while romantic love has a place to play in marriage, it is not the entire concept of love. Romantic love requires something more to sustain it. A marriage which tries to sustain itself upon romance will soon come up short. Couples who feel that this is what marriage is all about, soon find themselves drifting apart, convinced that they never were really "in love" because the feeling has gone, the thrill is over.

Storge — Fondness for One Another

In Romans 12:10, another form of love is mentioned. It is translated in our Bibles as "being kindly affectioned one toward another." It is used in Romans 1:31 and in 2 Timothy 3:3, where it is translated "without natural affection." This then is the love of family, the sense of belonging. It contains in it the idea of being devoted to one another. It has a sense of unconditional acceptance. It does not depend upon attainment or performance. It exists because of a relationship which already exists.

In marriage it might be thought of as the practical expression of the *agape* love idealized in marriage. It is a love which expresses oneness in outlook and goals. It abolishes competition between spouses. It creates not only a unity but an unconditional loyalty. Each upholds the other before the world (and more importantly before in-laws). The kind of trust and confidence that a husband has in his wife is expressed beautifully by Proverbs 31:11, "The heart of her husband doth safely trust in her." Also verse 28, "He praiseth her."

It was impressed on me years ago in college, when reading Robert Frost's poem, "The Death of the Hired Man," by his definition of home; "Home is the place where, when you have to go there, they have to take you in." It is belonging. That is the essence of *storge* love.This does not come with saying "I do" at the wedding ceremony. The Lord knew that each would crave it desperately in the relationship; He knew as well that it would take time to develop.

Yet even this love is not the goal or the totality of love in marriage. There are two more familiar words our New Testament employs.

Phileo — Friendship in Marriage

Friendship differs again from both *eros* and *storge*. In *eros*, two are occupied with each other. In *phileo* they are each occupied with some third thing. In *storge*, each accepts the other because of a relationship, a belonging to one another. In *phileo* each accepts the other because of the discovery or development of a mutual interest. Sharing is the key to this type of love. *Phileo* is the cherishing love enjoined upon the husband. Lest any think that somehow this is a deficient love or a love of less value than *agape*, bear in mind that the Father loves the Son with this same type of love (John 5:20). It is also used in 1 Corinthians 15:22 as the test of all true believers.

The husband and wife must work at this kind of love. Many of the mutual interests during courtship were indeed things which one did to please the other. With marriage, the focus sadly changes and most begin thinking about what they are receiving from the marriage. Doing something because a spouse enjoys it is now passed. Yet this love must be cultivated. For the Christian, there is certainly an excellent starting point as both should have the same spiritual interests. Other interests are certainly appropriate and necessary. The key here is on sharing them together and communicating.

Someone else has summarized this type of love as possessing three essential elements: comradeship, companionship, and communication. All must be cultivated carefully to produce the friendship so rewarding in married life.

Agape — The Fabric of Marriage

Space has been devoted to *agape* love in a previous article. It is important, however, to realize its relationship to the other loves already mentioned. *Agape* is more than all the other loves, an attitude rather than an emotion. Being such, it is not necessarily superior or more important than the others; it does, however, control and develop the others. It is the love which decides that I am going to love unconditionally, to share fully, to be permanently committed to my spouse. It is what controls *eros*, so that, in the words of another, "it does not become a god and destroy itself." It is what enables friendship to endure despite the failings of my spouse. It is the choosing not to see the shortcomings; it is 1 Corinthians 13 brought into a marriage.

If I might be allowed to quote at length one of the foremost christian writers of the twentieth century, "To say this (the need for *agape* love) is not to belittle the natural loves, but to indicate where their true glory lies. It is no disparagement to a garden to say that it will not fence and weed itself, nor prune its own fruit trees, nor roll and cut its own lawns. It will remain a garden, as distinct from a wilderness, only if someone does all these things to it." This is the roll which *agape* love plays in the marriage and its relationships to the other loves.

It is the husband's responsibility to nurture and

cultivate this love; he is to cheer up his wife. The idea is to delight and please. It is not a catering to whims or an indulging of materialistic desires. The word carries with it the idea of emotional satisfaction. The new husband must become a student of his wife and meet all her emotional needs. Unrealistic demands and demands that rival spiritual responsibilities are not in view.

The Intimacy of Marriage

One cannot read Deuteronomy 20:7; 24:5 without realizing God's intention for physical intimacy and enjoyment in marriage.

This is not a divine concession to human weakness. God did not "allow" physical enjoyment to pander to some lower, baser need in man. To use the words again of Deuteronomy 24:5 "he is to be free at home." These words carry with them the meaning of a clear conscience, the absence of guilt. Society has so debased sexual morality outside of marriage, that we at times have lost sight of its inherent purity within marriage.

This is part of that same first year responsibility. Intimacy includes the physical aspect, but is certainly much more. It involves emotional intimacy as well. Each sustains and reinforces the other. As the emotional intimacy grows in marriage, the physical joy increases as well. Young couples should not gauge their "love" by how exciting their romance is. In His infinite wisdom, God foresaw the need for a period of time of adjustment, of mutual education. This is still needed today.

It is obvious that the three principles, elaborated above, all build upon each other. Only as priority is given to marriage will a new husband be able to fulfill the responsibilities which the Word of God places upon him. Only in cultivating love in its four fold aspect, will he in turn be able to experience the true intimacy of marriage.

There are many things which potentially can disrupt the first year and thus the following years of marriage. These suggestions may sound out of step with modern thinking, but should be considered by newly married couples.

Learn to resolve differences without harboring resentment. "Let not the sun go down upon your wrath" (Eph. 4:26), is valid in marriage. There should be no areas which the two of you avoid speaking about because they are too emotional. Learn to resolve them patiently, together, and in the presence of God. Keep your problems between yourselves. Long after you have resolved them and forgotten them, those in whom you confided will remember.

Avoid debt at all costs. Over 75% of divorces in America have financial problems as a major contributing factor. Learn contentment with what God has given. Do not feel a need to have what other couples have. Hospitality is a matter of the size of the heart not the size of the home.

Never think of marriage as a 50-50 proposition. I frequently have to speak with young couples as part of a state requirement for marriage. I am surprised at the responses when I ask what each is doing now to avoid divorce after marriage. One young man recently said that they both realized that it was a 50-50 proposition. He was stunned when I said that it was more like 90-10. He would have to give 90% and only expect back 10%. It might be more scriptural for a husband to view it as 100%. Never go into marriage looking for what you can get back. It is a giving love which the husband is commanded to have.

It scarcely needs to be said, but it bears emphasis that no Christian couple should ever entertain separation or divorce. Any allowance of this as a legitimate option will completely undermine the application of scriptural principles to the problems which do arise in marriages. There must be an unconditional commitment of each partner to each other. Only then can problems be resolved using divine principles.

This article is really a plea to young married couples to give priority to their relationships. You must recognize that a wedding does not make a marriage. It simply gives you the chance to have a marriage. You must work at it diligently. The first year is only the beginning. It requires life long commitment to the divine principles of marriage to experience all that God intended.

CHAPTER FIVE

Heartbroken Homes (1)

"And they lived happily ever after" closes many a book but characterizes too few marriages. Yet the christian marriage has the potential to be the ideal that God intended. This by no means implies that it will be totally free of problems. It does mean that when problems arise they are dealt with in a way that leads to their resolution.

The Word of God is not silent about problems that can arise in marriage. Before we look at problem solving, it will be helpful to identify some of the problems and their sources from real life people as they make their way across the pages of Scripture. If, in reading these illustrations, there is any sense of identification, of *deja vu,* please be assured that you have begun the very first task in problem solving.

On the other hand, you do not have to find yourself in these examples from Scripture. You may already, being keenly aware of the pitfalls and dangers of married life, have taken steps to prevent problems. Yet seeing that marriage is the union of two imperfect individuals, we would all do well to take heed "lest we fall."

Nabal and Abigail

I have chosen to start with this little-appreciated

incident in the life of David because I believe it will serve to reveal the basic and yet ultimate problem which causes breaches in marriages, breaches that can become so wide that they seem for all purposes irremediable.

The key to appreciating the problem is the insight we are given by one of the servants as he reports to Abigail the exchange between Nabal and David's men. He says of Nabal, "He is such a son of Belial, that a man cannot speak to him" (1 Sam. 25:17). Now ask any wife, preferably your own, what is the greatest problem most men have, and she will most readily point to communication, or its lack. No one could speak to Nabal; not his wife, servants, or David's men.

Why this problem with communication? Fortunately, we are not left to conjecture. The same chapter gives us tremendous insights into its cause. The first trait that is obvious about this man is an exaggerated sense of self-importance. Notice, in verse 36, this petty herdsman treats himself like a king. Now add to this self imposed and self perpetuated ego trip what we have in verse 10, a genuine scorn for others, and we begin to see some of the elements which lead to poor communication. The final insight our chapter affords is when we see his stubborn nature in verses 10 and 11.

These may seem like severe traits to point out as a cause for failing to communicate. I ask only that you consider them. Communication is primarily, contrary to the thinking of many, a listening skill. Why do you listen to what someone has to say? Because you feel either the person or what they have to say is important. Nabal's sense of self importance and his scorn of others reveals that he thought no one else important. His stubbornness declared that nothing that anyone else thought was important. Can you identify to any degree here?

Communication between a husband and wife is essential. Any sense of superiority in the marriage, any ideas of self importance are unscriptural. Headship does not subjugate a spouse but elevates her. It assigns her and gives her a place of importance to the degree that a husband would lay down his life for his wife.

Lest any think that self importance is a sin that only the carnal are exposed to, be assured that it can wear sheep's clothing and infiltrate even the spiritual mind. When was the last time you were annoyed because what you were doing was so important, and your wife wanted to talk about "minor" things? When was the last time you were so "busy" with the household responsibilities and the children that you failed to notice your husband's spent appearance after a day at work? These may be only "little foxes" on the road to an exaggerated opinion of self and its duties, but they are the beginning.

Nabal manifests the full development of a stubborn personality. He is described, in verse 3, as being "churlish", or "hard" as the word really means. His days end under the hand of God when we are told that he became as stone. A hard man became as stone. An unwillingness to communicate carries with it the necessary ingredient for its own perpetuation.

If communication is so important, how can it be cultivated in a marriage? Is it more than just talking together at night? Is it a skill that is developed or a gift that one either has or never can have?

Communication can occur at several levels. Consider the usual, casual greetings that occur upon meeting someone. The "Hello," "How are you?" type of exchange would hardly be considered a very deep or meaningful form of communication. At the other end of the spectrum is the open and honest exposure of my thoughts, feelings and fears. The first reveals virtually nothing about me as a person; the latter reveals me totally. Therein lies the great problem. There is absolutely no risk in the first kind of exchange. The closer I get to the latter kind, the greater the risk becomes. This is why men find this type of exchange so difficult.

Allow me a brief diversion to highlight the point I am making. If you are a male reading this, what is your basic emotional desire? If you are a female, what is your basic need? Most men with insight recognize that a sense of importance, significance and value is what is essential to a sense of manliness. Women usually point to a need for emotional fulfillment, security, and relationships. It is the ego-emotion dichotomy, or as another has well termed it, the significance-security difference.

Now bring this essential difference back to the communication problem. A moment's reflection will show how everything is against the male and for the woman. To reveal my true self carries the risk of my spouse discovering weakness or failure in me. This would completely negate my sense of "significance." For a woman however, sharing her emotions is the goal which she seeks. It is no "failure" for her to be seen as she really is. She does not have as much of an investment in maintaining her ego as does her husband.

But help is near for this seeming impasse. The full orbed love the Scripture mandates in marriage allows both husband and wife to facilitate communication without fear of rejection. The believer's love transcends the world's not so much in quantity as in quality. It is a different kind of love. It is a love patterned after heaven's. This is the key.

Recall the problem which has arisen. The risk of communication lies in revealing myself and the discovery of weaknessses. Men fear that their wives may not really love or respect the person they really are. Yet all our imperfections and shortcomings are known to God. He has loved and continues to love despite what we are. The love which flourishes in marriage takes character from divine love, an unconditional acceptance of another. This should provide the secure atmosphere for both husband and wife to communicate without fear of rejection.

But a willingness to take the risk of communication does not guarantee success. It involves more than simply talking to or listening. The key element is in a mutual understanding of what is being said. Consider the exchange which occurred in John 8:21. The Lord Jesus warned the Jews, "Ye ... shall die in your sins: whither I go ye cannot come." This immediately led to speculation that the Lord was about to kill Himself. Was this misunderstanding because the Lord was attempting to be confusing?

Or doesn't it reveal one of the basic problems in attempts to communicate? We bring to bear upon every conversation and exchange of thought, a wealth of preconceived ideas and mind sets, prejudices and biases, if you will allow me to call them by their names. So that in hearing what someone says, I can hear what they are saying; I can think I hear what they really mean to say but are not saying directly; or I can selectively hear only what I want to hear. Sound confusing? It is and it makes communication very difficult. That's why it is imperative to develop an open and honest line of communication between a husband and wife. Each must say what they mean and each must hear what is being said.

One brief illustration may illuminate the point. Imagine the following incident: Your wife tells you that the recent hot humid weather has really been bothering her at home. That is what she said. But what will you hear? Some husbands will interpret her remarks to mean that she is complaining that they don't have an air conditioner in the living room. Another might think that what she means is that he is a failure in his job because they cannot afford a home at the shore. Another will view it as an attack upon his very person because he hasn't as yet had central air put in. Finally it is possible that she means simply that the hot humid weather is bothering her. The scenario that follows her statement will depend entirely upon which interpretation is made.

Because of its very nature, communication comes easier for a woman. Yet she is not without her inherent liability. Because she is more in touch with her emotions and by nature more sensitive, she may assume that her husband understands what she is trying to say even though she is couching it in vague language. She must strive to communicate on an open and rational level, not on an emotional level.

Forgive the rather lengthy discussion on communication. While more could be said, you will see the value of this art as we turn together to some of the other incidents recorded for us.

Rebekah and Isaac

One of the greatest tests and severest stresses in married life is children. It was just this test which Isaac and Rebekah failed. Genesis 27 chronicles the sad failure in their relationship. While this is not the section for dealing with principles of child rearing, this is the place to emphasize that children can cause a strain between husband and wife. Children especially in teen years are masters at playing parent against parent, of dividing and ruling.

Look at the details. The first thing which confronts us is a division between Isaac and Rebekah. There is a division in interest which quickly leads to a divergence in goals. Isaac loved Esau (Gen. 25:28) and Rebekah loved Jacob. From whence this division? Isaac liked the venison which Esau provided him, and Rebekah was closer to Jacob, a plain man who dwelt in tents (v. 27). To put this in simpler terms, they both had their favorite because of something which appealed to them about the person. These may seem like minor things, but many a parent has showed favoritism to a child because of a resemblance or natural talent that bears a likeness to the parent, some trait that appeals to the pride in the parent soon leads to special status that causes a divergence in goals for that child from those of the spouse.

In Genesis 27, the division soon led to a distance between Isaac and Rebekah. Each is going his own way to devise blessing for the "favorite." Neither consults with the other, but cloaked in secrecy, works out their own plan.

Anything which separates partners can only lead to greater problems in a marriage. If the raising of children has led to a conflict between husband and wife, it is essential to resolve the issue. Each parent going his or her own way will only deepen the problem, resulting in tragedy.

To accomplish ends, Rebekah must resort to deceitfulness. Her act is born in deceit and requires additional twisting of truth at the end (v. 46) to cover her act. No insight is given as to whether Isaac recognized Rebekah's behind-the-scenes manoeuvring or not. If so, what a blow to the mutual trust that undergirds marriage! If he did not, how tragic that Rebekah had to live with the knowledge of deceiving her own husband!

Most tragic of all is the disappointment that followed all their separate ideas. Isaac did not give the blessing to Esau as he had planned; though Jacob did get the blessing, Rebekah never saw him again. She died with the awareness of Esau's hatred for his brother and the threat to kill Jacob engraved in her soul.

Every stress can have the result of either dividing or uniting a marriage. The challenge of raising children in a humanistic society, with pressures from every conceivable area being brought to bear upon parents, should drive them closer to each other and closer to the Lord. How essential that unity should mark the parents before the children! It is incumbent upon parents to avoid any "behind the back" dealing with children as though this will gain them favour and leverage. A unified front is imperative.

CHAPTER SIX

Heartbroken Homes (2)

Jacob and Rachel

If communication was the nemesis in Nabal's and Abigail's marriage, and if children were the strain between Isaac and Rebekah, then competition and compatibility problems beset Jacob and his favorite wife.

The incident is well known in Genesis 30:1. Jacob has begotten children through Leah but not through Rachel. In a fit of envy, Rachel exclaimed, "Give me children or else I die!" The Scriptures point out that this was because of envy. Her desire then had an unholy source; it was born of envy, a desire to have what another had.

Many a marriage has been ruined upon the rocks of competition. Young couples marry, mortgage themselves and their futures, become indebted for material things, all with a view to having what others have. What they fail to realize is that it may have taken others years to get the very same things, which they in turn would like to get overnight. It is currently estimated that well over half of the divorces in the USA today have money problems as a major source of discord. Many times indebtedness occurs and each blames the other. Goals and priorities are not set; budgets are unheard of; gratification must be instantaneous; delay in having is looked upon as failure.

Couples contemplating marriage should discuss financial matters and have a clear understanding of their resources and limits. We live in a society which is geared to credit buying and debt. The young believer especially must avoid this early in marriage.

Not only was her desire from a wrong motive but her demand was in a wrong direction. As Jacob rightly answered, "Am I in God's stead..." She was blaming her husband instead of taking the circumstances from the Lord. How different were Isaac and Rebekah (Gen. 25:21) who entreated the Lord and received fruit as a result.

Spouses look in the wrong direction at times. Just as Rachel did. Husbands blame wives and wives in turn blame husbands, because they don't have what others have. One accuses the other of poor budgeting; the other is blamed for failure to move ahead in the job. Soon a decision is reached for both to work and to defer the family until things are "better" financially. This is not a condemnation of women working; it is a condemnation if it is just to keep up with others and have more material goods to call our own. Even the secular world and sociologists have taken note of the vast effects that women in the work force have caused. It has changed family life, society and marriages.

Finally in considering Rachel, it is obvious that her device for solving the problem was also wrong. In attempting to keep up with others, in accusing her husband of failure, she resorted to an expediency tha really did not satisfy her. In struggling to have what others do, we learn to our loss that having does not satisfy. Even more tragically, the woman who cried, "Give me children or else I die," received both parts of her threat. In giving birth to Benjamin, her second child, she died.

But Rachel and Jacob introduce an additional problem. Recognizing that some unique differences exist because of the multiplicity of wives which Jacob had, there were nevertheless some problems of compatibility between Rachel and Jacob. These are detailed for us in chapter 30:14-18.

Problems in the physical sphere do arise in marriage. Frequently they are the result of wrong expectations. Courtship with all of its emotional elements which are constantly being held in check gives rise to unrealistic expectations in marriage. The restraints are now withdrawn and couples expect immediate and permanent ecstacy. When expectations are not fulfilled, a spouse may withdraw and interpret this as a lack of "love," a lack of the "real thing." Reverse reasoning may lead one of the spouses to wonder if they are really "in love," equating the emotional experience with *agape* love.

Husbands and wives must display patience and understanding in this most intimate area of marriage. A husband would not accuse his wife of lack of love if she burned the dinner. A wife would not question the depth of her husband's love if he failed in his first wall papering job. Both would recognize the need for experience and time. Why be less patient in the most emotional, intimate, and (contrary to popular press) least natural aspects of marriage. The physical response is a very individual one and both husband and wife must learn how to satisfy each other. It does not come naturally.

Moses and Zipporah

In the brief glimpse which we are afforded into the husband and wife relationship of Moses and Zipporah, there is an incident which reveals one of the great spoilers of marriage: compromise. We are not referring here to each giving a bit, relative to their own rights. It is compromise of principle that is involved here.

Look at the details for a moment. In the land of Midian, Moses finds a wife. God graciously grants them two sons (Ex. 4:20) while there. He is called by God to return to Egypt. He departs with his wife and sons; he stops by the way in an inn where the strangest conceivable event takes place. We are informed that the Lord met him and sought to kill him. Follow closely what ensues. Zipporah took a sharp stone and cut off the foreskin of her son, not her sons. In frustration she casts it at Moses' feet with the epithet, "A bloody husband art thou to me."

What does all this mean? If circumcision was so important to God, why was only one son involved? It appears that Moses and Zipporah reached a family crisis with the birth of two sons. Moses, the Hebrew, doubtless argued for circumcision. To Zipporah, this was abhorrent. How was the problem resolved? By compromise. Obviously one son was circumcised to please Moses, and one was left uncircumcised to please Zipporah. Everyone was happy but God. In reality no one was happy. Her accusation to Moses proves that she was angry at the compromise and at being forced to be the circumcisor of her son.

There must be room for compromise in a marriage. The room however should involve amoral and nonscriptural issues. Compromise over the colour of the wallpaper, but not over divine principles.

Sadly we can sometimes agree on the former issues and not on the latter. There should be no compromise relative to clearly revealed principles from God. Zipporah reluctantly, but finally obeyed God. In doing so, she virtually blames Moses. Neither partner came out ahead. Both lost.

When differences do arise over scriptural things, they must be resolved together in the presence of God. When Paul was dealing with Euodias and Syntyche (Phil 4:2, not a marriage relationship I know, but grant me this liberty), he does not take sides or suggest compromise on a middle ground. He advocates being of the same mind in the Lord. Submit all differences to the principle of the Lordship of Christ and take what comes from that even if it means loss (Phil. 4:5).

Job and His Wife; Hannah and Elkanah

I almost hesitate to mention these worthies as being guilty of failure. There is little if anything which can be said against them.

There is, however, an incident in both marriages which reveals a lack. When Hannah was mourning over Israel's condition and her lack of a son to give to God, Elkanah did not realize the depth of her sorrow and wondered why Hannah was so grieved. He actually took it personally, as though somehow Hannah wanted a son more than a husband.

When Job was going through his severe trial, which his wife shared in large measure, she advised him to "curse God and die."

Elkanah was guilty of a lack of sensitivity to his wife's need. Mrs. Job was likewise culpable of a lack of support to her husband in his hour of need.

This reflects back upon the basic differences in men and women. Men tend to be short on the sensitivity of others; we fall into the trap of taking the emotional lows of our wives personally. Women likewise fail to support and nurture the fragile "ego" of their husbands, responding only on an emotional level.

Abram and Sarai

Heartache and sadness marred Abram's marriage because of a collapse in headship. This is something further away from God's ideal than even compromise. He abdicated his role as head and allowed his wife to make decisions. In Genesis 16, the long trial of barrenness finally wears upon Sarai, and she suggests a way for Abram to have children through Hagar. Abram harkened to his wife's advice. Envy, hatred, bitterness and strife were born into the home as well as the child, Ishmael. When Sarai complains that Abram should never have listened to her bad advice to begin with, Abram again resolves the problem by giving his wife the responsibility for decision making, "Thy maid is in thy hand; do to her as it pleaseth thee." In other words, you take over and do as you please.

The immediate and long range tragedy from this shortsighted advice is familiar to every reader. Although Sarai was out of place, the ultimate blame lies with Abram for abdicating leadership.

In every sphere of life, we are accustomed to a central authority. Without it we become insecure and ill at ease. Few would wish to enter a city or state in which there was no one "in charge." We all know that the natural tendencies of men must be kept in check by the consciousness, and at times the presence, of authority.

In a similar manner, headship must be maintained in a family if all is to be in order and harmonious. Its absence will lead to an "every man doing what is right in his own eyes" condition. This is equivalent to nothing being right or wrong. Whatever the challenge and whatever the cost, a husband must maintain headship according to divine standards.

David and Michal

This tragic marriage witnessed what has been the death blow to many relationships. As David returned from the house of Obed-edom with the ark, we are told that he danced before the Lord with all his might, girded with a linen ephod. Michal who is discerningly called Saul's daughter, not David's wife, saw him and despised him in her heart. When he returned to his house, she verbally attacked and berated him.

It is clear that Michal loved the manly warrior of 1 Samuel 17 and 18, exalted to be king in 2 Samuel 3, but the pious, humble man of this chapter is beneath her dignity and pride. She is rightly called Saul's daughter. She obviously had a love for externals, place, accomplishment and honor. She exaggerates in her condemnation of David, charging him with uncovering himself before the handmaidens as he danced. Scripture clearly says he was dressed with a linen ephod. She degrades him verbally by scorn and ridicule. She attacks him at his most sensitive point, his self esteem. Her attack was meant to destroy. Were David anything less than a spiritual man, she might well have succeeded.

Michal's behaviour illustrates some especially important dangers in discussing differences. She attacked David. When a problem or difference surfaces, never attack the spouse; always attack the problem. Face it honestly, being aware of why it bothers you. Seek for solutions, not simply majoring on the problem.

Marriages rise and fall on mutual esteem and trust. Guard jealously these values. Eschew anything which would introduce the opposite into your marriage.

Hosea and Gomer

The ultimate strain upon any marriage is seen in the heart rending story of Hosea and his wayward wife, Gomer. Infidelity is the worst stress which a marriage can be called upon to endure. What is most remarkable in this scriptural incident is that the problem does appear to have been all one sided. The fault lay squarely upon Gomer and not in any measure upon Hosea.

The great lesson to be learned here is the kind of home to which Gomer returned. It is remarkable that the three prodigals in our Bible all met the same thing at the front door.

In closing this article with Gomer and Hosea I am not so much pleading for a solution to the hurt of infidelity, as a solution to all the hurt and misunderstandings which occur in marriage. In this closest of all human relationships, there is great potential for problems. It is almost axiomatic that the more potential good there is in something, the more potential evil there is if things go out of control. The fence which surrounds marriage, the foundation which upholds it, the atmosphere which pervades it, must include this type of love which can forgive without reserve or condition.

CHAPTER SEVEN

Luke's Family-Life Series

Long before the current plethora of writings on marriage and the family (I suppose I am also guilty here now), there came from the Spirit of God, through the pen of a first century physician, a brilliant series on marriage and the family. The case histories and vignettes were not labeled as such, but rather interwoven through the fabric of his delightful unfolding of the perfect Man. The lessons learned are valuable and insightful even for us over nineteen centuries later. Let any of us who are tendering new advice remember that God has already given it through Luke 2000 years ago.

We have, we trust with divine aid and to our mutual profit, traced God's pattern for marriage in the last several articles. Before us lies the vast and critical matter of family life. It is hoped that this article will serve as a bridge between the two already intimately related subjects.

Allow your mind the freedom to return to a Greek medical school and a young student known to us as Luke. His early training, in accordance with the principles of that day of medical training, would stress the importance of careful observation and detailed history taking. His skills as an observer and collator of facts would be sharpened razor fine during time spent with the great teachers of his day. In an age when remedies were few, great stress was placed upon the ability to diagnose by observation and listening.

It takes little imagination to realize that the Spirit of God picked up this young physician with these skills and, after conversion, used them in the writing of the most touching and tender of the gospel accounts. Note how Luke himself states that he had "accurate understanding" from above (Luke 1:3). Doubtless time was spent with Mary, questioning the early days of the Lord's life, His boyhood, and early years. We owe a great debt to Luke for the touches that come from his pen as he paints upon the canvas of Holy Scripture, the scenes of the Lord's life. The idea of the "understanding" which Luke professed to have is the knowledge that is the result of a thorough investigation. This was no haphazard collection of tales and rumors.

Luke writes with definite human interest. His Gospel is replete with accounts of widows and women, rich men and rogues, tears and touches, prayers and praises, fellowship at tables and family life. It is especially the latter element which is before us at this time. It is indeed refreshing to turn from the examples of the shortcomings in married life which have occupied us in previous articles to consider some of the virtues as seen in married couples which are described by Luke's pen.

We are introduced in the very first chapter of Luke's Gospel to a couple who epitomize many of the highest ideals of married life. They lived in the days of Herod, days marked by something less than the most moral of ethics. They were days when, as each of the synoptic writers tell us, theologians argued about divorce in an attempt to legitimize personal desires. Stable, monogamous marriage had given way to serial monogamy. The court of Herod was not renowned for morality. An heir to the throne would blatantly take his own brother's wife. Yet amidst this atmosphere, there is a couple who are characterized as righteous, blameless, yet barren. Their marriage was according to the Word of God, which required the Levite to marry within his tribe (ch. 1:5). While it is difficult if not impossible to summarize each of the three marriages described by Luke in one word, we could write over their marriage; harmony, headship, and a heavy burden.

This aged and honourable couple, Zacharias and Elizabeth, had together lived and shared life's blessings and burdens. Upon their hearts, and perhaps most heavily upon the heart of Elizabeth, had weighed the great reproach of barrenness. Their journey through life had been marked by personal sadness. Like the two walkers, whose story closes Luke's Gospel, they had doubtless lost hope (Luke 24:21). Despite personal righteousness, the barrenness of their marriage had caused reproach for them before the nation.

To this faithful priest a divine messenger is sent winging his way to earth. "Thy prayer is heard," may have reference to their personal prayer for a son, or it may refer to Zacharias' position as priest, praying for the nation and its deliverance. Whichever view is taken, it is obvious that as a wise and considerate husband he had shared the burden of years of personal sorrow with his wife. He had learned to be supportive, tender, and understanding.

Notice some of the touches which the Spirit of God adds: in v. 40, it is "the house of Zacharias"; in vs. 60-63, it is evident that they were in agreement as to the name of the child. Despite being stricken dumb, he had been able to communicate with his wife concerning this important matter. She gladly allows his word to be the final authority in the matter. As our first chapter in Luke closes, the curtain falls on a married couple who, indeed, have enjoyed what Peter later called "the grace of life." In some hill country, in some city in Judah, we picture this venerable couple closing out their days together with the echo of Zacharias' last recorded words in their ears, "the way of peace."

The first two chapters of Luke also introduce us to Mary and Joseph. Luke, as is his custom, seems to dwell primarily on Mary. Matthew's account, which stresses the Lord's legal right to the throne of Israel, emphasizes Joseph's role. Yet, even in Luke's account, it is touching to consider them. It is obvious that Joseph was all Mary had on the earthly level. He is seen taking her under his care despite what must have meant great personal reproach and cost. *Agape* love was evidenced in them to a high degree. He was seeing to her welfare despite what it would cost him. He is her protector and guide. He is with her in the journey (vs. 4, 5), with her through the birth (v. 16), with her in fulfilling her responsibilities to the law and the journey to Jerusalem (v. 22), and the return trip to Nazareth (v. 39). At no stage does he forsake her for more "important" things.

Their home was also marked by a very definite desire to give the Lord priority in spiritual things. We are told that the parents went up every year to Jerusalem at the feast of passover (v. 41). Keep in mind that these were not wealthy landowners, Joseph and Mary were from the working class. A journey to Jerusalem was costly, and there was no vacation pay for a self employed carpenter. But God came first in their lives. Obedience and harmony in the spiritual realm are essential in marriage.

A small but touching incident is found even amidst Mary's mistake. When she and Joseph finally found their missing child in the Temple, Mary's well intentioned but incorrect rebuke was, "Thy father and I have sought thee sorrowing." She gave prominence to Joseph even here. This may seem minor, but how often we think of our own anxiety and sorrow first, even ahead of our spouse's.

It is from Luke's pen that we first hear and learn of Priscilla and Aquila. To be sure, Paul will enlarge our knowledge of them, yet Luke introduces us to them and gives us a lasting first impression. Comments have been made upon this couple in a previous article but allow me the liberty of just noting, from Acts 18, their hospitality to Paul and then to Apollos. It is little wonder that this grace grew until it embraced the local church (1 Cor. 16:19), and then all the churches of the Gentiles (Rom. 16:3, 4). This underlines an important principle for married couples: do what God brings into your life and the Lord will increase your sphere of usefulness.

Their move to Corinth was little more than

bowing to the powers that be. Yet once there, a service for God became obvious. Having discharged this, they purchased a good degree and great boldness in the faith. Doors of opportunity opened and their service became valuable to all the churches.

But turn now for a few moments to consider something of family life in Luke. I would like to underline two families. The first was marked by a perfect Son; the latter by a perfect father.

Family life in Nazareth must have been very difficult. A village from which no good thing could come would hardly be the place for raising children. Yet here was where the Word of God directed Joseph and Mary. The unlikely soil of Nazareth witnessed the most unique growth that has ever occurred. In one sense it was very natural, yet in another sense it was most unnatural.

Notice first, however, a few details concerning Mary and Joseph. We are told that Mary "pondered (these things) in her heart" (2:19), and again, "His mother kept all these sayings in her heart" (2:51). I learn from these, and other Scriptures, the essential need to become students of our children. I recognize fully the unique nature of this child, and also the unusual character of her meditations. Yet the principle is of value to note. We must take time and learn to observe the strengths and weaknesses (He had none) of our children if we are going to help them to develop. More on this later.

Joseph does not get much further mention in our gospel account. There are two inferences, however, that must not pass us by. As has been mentioned,

Joseph went up to the feast year by year. Also, we are informed that the Lord went into the synagogue on the sabbath "as His custom was" (4:16). When had these godly habits begun? We all know that the Lord would have manifested these on His own, yet the point here is that Josesph had taught his family to develop habits that put God first. It had been Joseph's custom to recognize spiritual responsibilities; his children followed his godly example. It is rare for children to rise higher than their parents in their establishing of priorities. Parents who have failed to be at the assembly gatherings on a consistent basis, scarce need ask if their children will deem it important to be at all the gatherings.

Allow me to stray to Matthew and Mark for one point. In Matthew 13:55, we are told that Joseph was a carpenter. In Mark 6:3, the Lord Jesus is referred to as "the carpenter." Joseph had evidently taught Him the trade, preparing Him for future years. He wisely established goals and training for the lad. I realize that the Son was unique and had eternal goals and purposes. Yet Joseph must be commended on the human family level for taking care for his family's future. This leads into the final point I would like to make concerning the Lord's early years at Nazareth.

Recall the difficult verse with which Luke 2 ends: "And Jesus increased in wisdom and stature, and in favor with God and man." I am not now going to attempt to explain all the questions which some have with this verse. That task will fall to abler minds and more eloquent pens. Simply allow me to show that there are four areas of development for which I, as a parent, am responsible. "He increased in wisdom," suggests the emotional and intellectual side of life. "Stature" is the physical aspect. "Favour with God" is the spiritual element. "With man" underlines the social development. May I say something that all may not agree with immediately? I believe not only that I have a responsibility for all these spheres, but that it is an equal responsibility in them all. It is obvious is it not that you must provide for the physical growth of a child? While we place an emphasis on the spiritual side of growth because it has the greatest consequences, you would not feel successful as a parent if your child were malnourished and sickly, but able to recite verse after verse. You willingly own a responsibility for his physical as well as spiritual welfare. In just the same way, we are accountable for the emotional and social adjustment of our children. If you question this, consider for a moment how the spiritual side may be forever marred by a warping of the social or emotional aspect. We must channel these and control them with a view to spiritual welfare and usefulness, but we dare not neglect them. To impair the social adjustment of a child by unnecessary isolation and over regulation may forever hinder his ability to speak to men for God or even to get along with his brethren.

Turn in closing to the perfect father in Luke 15. Here was a father who had ably provided for his own. A day came when a son wanted to leave home. He was willing to let him go and endure the pain. To his credit, when his son was many miles distant both physically and morally, there were impressions that had been made that never left. The son knew and remembered a well ordered home, but he not only knew his father's home, he knew his father's heart. He knew his father well enough to know that he could at least expect mercy and reception.

What will our children remember of us when they leave home? What impressions have been made during the eighteen or more years that God has entrusted them to us? Do they know us well enough to know what to expect from us. This kind of knowledge does not come easily or quickly. It involves cost, not only of time but of emotions. The willingness to hear in order to be heard; the grace to acknowledge that, perhaps as a parent, I have been wrong or too hasty in a judgment. All this enables our children to know us and to have confidence in us.

The father had an open door for his son. You may well add that it was upon his terms, not the son's. That is true, yet, to his everlasting credit, it must be shown that he patiently waited despite a heart that must have been heavy with sorrow and care. Compassion, love, forgiveness and grace were all in abundance in that parabolic home. No need for "I told you so," undue harshness or warnings as to the future. Here was a father who had perfect timing. He did not break the bruised reed; nor did he quench the dimly burning wick.

Even in dealing with the elder son in the field, the father manifested traits which we as parents should strive to emulate. He was patient and entreated his son. He went out to him. He did not stand on ceremony. He was not afraid of "losing face" or appearing soft. Despite profligate living on the part of one son, and proud words from another, this father never lost control. He only lost control at the reception back of his prodigal son. He broke down with tears of joy and kisses of forgiveness.

It is essential to be in control with our children. Neither discipline nor kindness must be from a posture of anger or weakness. The welfare of our children must be paramount.

You may well be able to add to this brief consideration from Luke's writings. The length of the article is not as important as its lessons. May we, like Zacharias and Elizabeth, live life together, sharing its burdens and blessings. May we have grace, like Joseph and Mary, to be united in its experiences, and supportive one to another in its trials. The perfect father of Luke 15 is before us, not so much to remind us of shortcomings, but to serve as a goal. Mary's insightful study of her Son, and Joseph's concern for the spiritual and social development of his family, can all serve as examples for us.

CHAPTER EIGHT

On Being Single

Society at large still places great stress upon marriage. The "ideal" life is still composed of a family, two children, car, home, and other affordable luxuries. Security and success, accomplishment and acceptance seem inextricably linked in thinking with marriage. Perhaps even more than society, the assemblies place great emphasis upon marriage. The stress in most assemblies is on couples. The worth of a woman is frequently linked with her husband and his role. Many assembly activities are centered around home and family life.

The single life has some very difficult hurdles to overcome. Many begin to look upon themselves as rejected, unwanted, and somehow not up to the level of acceptability which others have experienced. A real loss of sense of worth, of value, and of purpose in life may beset the single person. June can be a very traumatic time emotionally as others your age marry and walk off hand in hand into the future. Conferences can sadly become only repeat exercises in frustration and rejection as hopes for friendship and the future are left unfulfilled.

When we come to the Scriptures, we are faced with a problem. The Lord Jesus spoke of those who were destined to a single life because they were so "born from their mother's womb"; of others, who were single because they were "made eunuchs by men," and of others still who were single "for the kingdom of God's sake" (Matt. 19:12). The difficulty which we face is that although a few Christians may choose not to marry for the kingdom of God's sake, most of the single Christians, with whom we are all associated, do not fit into any of the above categories. For many the problem centres around a lack of available partners. Though some young men may not be able to find suitable partners, it is largely our sisters who, because of the relative imbalance between young men and women, fail to find a partner. Single men and single women do however have separate distinct situations. If this article gives the bulk of the attention to single women, it is because they experience more of the problems and are more prevalent amongst us.

What help can the Scriptures give us on this? Are we to relegate this all to that area of the silence of Scriptures? I firmly believe that the Word of God has answers and guidance for us all in this difficult and emotionally troubling area. It is imperative however that we clear away some well intentioned but harmful concepts.

How are we to view those who have not married? At times expressions such as "unclaimed gems," "monuments to the stupidity of the brethren" and "unfulfilled lives," are used. These terms are employed in an attempt to convey that the single person is truly worthwhile, although not married. While these terms may be used with good intention, they are harmful, wrong, and above all unscriptural. They serve notice to all that something is amiss; they suggest that being single is abnormal, a disease that only afflicts abnormal people.

Think of the subtle implication in the use of these expressions. Are single people really unclaimed treasures? Why can't they be viewed as useful treasures to others even in their single state? The God who made them and who controls their lives has brought about this circumstance as it has pleased Him. To say that a single sister is a "monument to the stupidity of the brethren" is to imply that a gross mistake has been made; that the failure of a brother somewhere, has led to a sister being consigned to a single life. This implies that God's will has gone awry and all is out of order.

Would you suggest that things are out of God's control to someone who has lost a loved one? Would you confront any major circumstance in a person's life in that fashion? Being single may very well be the will of God for some individuals. This does not make the unique problems of singleness any less trying, but it does offer a great comfort to those who are single.

How are we to view the single state? How should a single person view herself and her circumstances?

At times, while being single is a choice, it is spoken of as a sacrifice. What is meant is that out of obedience to the Word of God, single individuals refuse the interest and invitations of those either not saved, or those with whom they feel a relationship would be out of the mind of God. The essence of ALL obedience is sacrifice, the sacrifice of my will to God's. Yet this sacrifice never entails a true loss. We cannot then look upon this in a totally negative way.

Being unmarried is a circumstance ordered by God in one's life. It is perhaps one of the most important circumstances which God brings into a person's life. Most will not view it as ideal, even though Paul, in 1 Corinthians 7, does emphasize some of its advantages. It is granted then that it is a problem for those who would desire to marry but have not the opportunity. The problem of singleness enlarges to embrace the added difficulties of loneliness, frustrated hopes, loss of self-esteem, unfulfilled desires for intimacy, and required independence. Many unmarried individuals could add to the list.

It may sound naively simple to some, but if a Christian faces a problem, the answer is found in the Lord. This is not a sublimation of which the psychologist speaks: the redirecting of intense physical desires into the spiritual realm. This is far more than simply being so occupied with one area of life that the other is forgotten. It is certainly not merely a way of receiving comfort for the self pity which might engross the unmarried. It is an answer, not a patching up; it is a solution, not an anesthetic.

It is imperative for the unmarried person to come to grips with his circumstances as being the Lord's will for him at that particular time in his life. If the single person desires marriage, he can certainly look for it in the future. But Paul's words at which we will look, in 1 Corinthians 7, will have little profit if the all compelling thought is marriage. There is no loss in waiting upon God for a partner. The time is well invested in coming to an understanding of God's will and in arriving at values which you would look for in a partner and which you would bring to a marriage. A young sister's recent comment speaks far more eloquently than my writing, "I shudder to think of the men that attracted me when I was younger."

When Paul took up his pen to write to the Corinthians, he was writing to an assembly whose testimony was set amidst an immoral society. Lust and immorality had reached epidemic proportions and no one was calling for vaccines against them. So depraved was the society that men coined the term "Corinthianize" to express moral decadence. Newly saved saints at Corinth would understandably question the place which marriage and physical intimacy had in the Christian life. This is one of the themes which Paul takes up in chapter 7.

There is much of profit in vs. 1-16; most of this applies to marriage and its several problems. Continuing down the chapter to vs. 17-24 we are confronted with

Principles of Devoted Living

One of the principles which Paul underlines in this paragraph is the necessity to **appreciate** the value which God has placed on you. "Ye are bought with a price" (v. 23). Every child of God is of value in the estimation of God. We must never confuse our unworthiness with the idea of worthlessness. Whether single or married, every individual and every life is of importance to God. This is one of the points which Paul is stressing in this section.

Thoughts of self pity and personal rejection must be refused and replaced by an appreciation of my worth before the Lord.

In this light, we must honestly face a problem which single individuals face. The manner in which married people view, treat and refer to single people frequently reinforces their sense of low self esteem. There are **no** second class saints, only second class thinkers. Every child is of value to God and should be of value to those who wish to think as God does.

Notice also the need to **accept** whatever circumstances into which God has brought us. Some were questioning their relationships both in marriage and society now that they were converted. Paul emphasizes "Let every man abide in the same calling wherein he was called" (v. 20). This applies equally to those who find themselves single. There is no need to feel that somehow things are out of God's control, that you will never really reach God's goal for your life until you are married. Paul moves to this in the next verse in which he stresses the need to **avail** yourself of every opportunity where you are to serve God. Notice verse 21, "Art thou called being a servant? Care not for it: but if thou mayest be made free, rather use it." To paraphrase loosely verses 21 and 22, "Don't become the slave of circumstances or of other people."

Many sit along the sidelines waiting for marriage as the ticket into Christian life and service for God. Self pity, a lack of self confidence, a misunderstanding about God's purposes all may combine to paralyze a person. Paul makes clear that all saints should seek to serve God where they are and in whatever circumstances they are found. Is it too much to apply this to being single? If you are seeking to please and honour God in your life and walking according to His will, you are not now receiving "second best." Don't even wait for marriage to get involved in life itself. A full, rich, meaningful life is within your grasp, if you are in the will of God.

Later in the article we will look together at some single individuals in the Scriptures and their activity. The point to be stressed now is that life does not begin with marriage; it begins with conversion. Seek opportunities to serve God. It may come as a surprise to some to realize that being single does have some advantages. I recognize that many who would desire to be married would freely trade these "advantages" for some of the "hardships" of marriage. But God has placed you there now and given you, perhaps only temporarily, these advantages. Few single people realize the demands which married life places on a person's time. This is even after we extract the romanticized element from marriage. Responsibilities and demands mount with the passing of time and the arrival of children. Single people have far more time to devote to the Lord and to others. The years prior to marriage, even if protracted, are a valuable time for growth and appreciation of the Lord. A woman has few opportunities to learn dependence upon the Lord if she goes immediately from the relationship of a dependent child in the home to a dependent wife in the family.

Finally, Paul makes a plea that every saint should

use whatever circumstances God has brought him into, to **abide** with God (v. 24). Cultivating the fellowship of God is something which is open to every believer in every set of circumstances.

The Priority of Divine Things

The eternal abiding principles of God transcend cultures, time and circumstances. Paul brings us to one of these great truths in a somewhat roundabout fashion in verse 29, "But this I say, brethren, The time is short." Paul has really put the teachings of the Lord Jesus in Matthew 6:33 in a somewhat updated version, "Seek ye first the Kingdom of God and His righteousness; and all these things shall be added unto you." Keep in mind the context in which the Lord spoke these words. He was rebuking the anxious, covetous spirit of the day. His words are still applicable today; putting God first and allowing Him to order the remainder of my life will never result in loss.

A word of caution must be introduced here. This does not mean that if I put God first He will give me a partner in life. The Lord Jesus is speaking about the necessities of life; what a man will need to live and serve God. If the Lord feels you need a partner, He will provide that partner in His time. In the meanwhile, put God first. Don't become so distracted by the search and longing for a partner that your service for God becomes sidetracked.

Some pray for a partner using the words of Matthew 7:7, "Ask and it shall be given unto you," as a credo. But heaven is not a branch office of

Sears. We don't simply put in our order and demand next day shipment. All is subject to His will.

One of the underlying reasons that Paul subjugates even marriage to the spiritual priority of serving God is that even marriage is only temporary. Our relationship and service with God is eternal. How tragic to put the priority on the temporal and passing things (v. 31), only to become unfulfilled in the eternal.

Many Scriptures rush to mind to support the need for all, single and unmarried, to carefully survey their circumstances and to use all for God. Ephesians 5:15 counsels us to redeem the time.

Paul has one more major point to make in this section which does have a bearing upon our discussion. In verses 32-40, he touches upon

The Pattern of a Directed Life

Paul's great desire (v. 32), was to have everyone serving the Lord without distraction. For him, the single life had this advantage. This may not be the case for all; Paul owns this freely. It was however an advantage for him.

Afford me the freedom for a moment to illustrate this principle from the lives of some of the best known saints in our Bibles. Some may well have been single all their lives; others had important events prior to marriage which are worthwhile noting.

Virtually synonymous with hospitality are the names of Mary and Martha. Their hospitality put Bethany on the map. It became known as the "town of Mary and Martha" (John 12:1). Here then were two sisters who did not sit back and await the future to unfold. They saw a need and addressed themselves to it. Hospitality to the Lord and His followers became their ministry. All that the Lord and His disciples needed was to be found at this home in Bethany. It was not merely a meal which was provided. Martha saw to the natural needs of the body; Lazarus to the emotional needs of social life and fellowship, and Mary to spiritual life. This does not imply anything about the relative spirituality of the three. It only teaches that hospitality with them was all inclusive.

Your single state does not prohibit you from entertaining the Lord's people and making your home a spiritual haven. This may not always be possible. It will depend on living arrangements. If it is possible however, go in for it. Wisdom and care are needed, but the opportunities are boundless and the rewards are incalculable.

Dorcas graces the pages of our Bibles only briefly in a short account in Acts 9:36-43. What is prominent in her service is that she was occupied for others. So noted was she for her selfless character, that she is the only woman in our Bibles called a disciple. She followed the pattern of the Lord Jesus who poured out His life for others (Phil. 2:3-8). Famous for her good deeds and life for those less fortunate, she became a one woman welfare and social security office for the widows. Here was a woman who was not distracted by other responsibilities and could give herself wholly to the needs of others.

Phoebe, servant of the church at Cenchrea, has been immortalized upon the pages of Scripture by the deft pen of the Spirit of God. Marked by a genuine interest in the assembly and a generous attitude toward all, she has remained a pattern of how much good a sister can do in her God given sphere. The words which the Spirit has chosen to use suggest that through personal exercise and expense she had been a help to Paul and to the assembly at Cenchrea. Being single can allow for more financial support to the work of God and the people of God.

Paul and Timothy appear to have used their unmarried and single status as an opportunity to serve the Lord without the distractions of married life. The demands made upon their time by the Spirit of God would have been almost impossible for a family man to have fulfilled.

These lives should suffice to illustrate that the essence of life, that which really matters, is not dependent upon marital status. Self esteem, service for God, and communion with God are independent of marriage. It is your attitude, not your marital state which will determine these.

A brief examination of some Old Testament lives also affords some valuable insights into the unique problems and solutions of the single life.

The life of Jeremiah is almost a commentary upon the phrase which Paul employed in 1 Corinthians 7:26, "I suppose that this is good for the present distress." I can almost hear someone groaning at the mention of Jeremiah. "Singleness and sobs," the "lonely prophet and the lamenter." How appropriate!

What comfort could a single person derive from his life?

In Jeremiah 16:1-3, he is forbidden by God to marry. Some are quick to add that God only said "in this place," meaning Jerusalem. It appears however that Jeremiah never married. His ministry and stand for God was characterized by loneliness. In chapter 15:17, he lamented that he sat alone because of the Word of God. In chapter 16, he discovered that he must also live alone because of the same Word. He never knew what it was to come home from a long day at the court and have the sympathy of a wife. He never had the privilege of sharing his burden and grief over spiritual conditions with a helpmeet. Lonely days were followed by lonely nights.

Jeremiah was called to learn God amidst his circumstances (Jer. 15:20, 21). He was a forerunner of the one who said, "I have learned in whatsoever state I am to be content; ... I am strong for all things in Christ who is constantly pouring strength into me" (Phil. 4:11, 13).

Daniel affords us valuable lessons on the single life. Doubtless made eunuchs by men, Daniel and his three friends did not wallow in self pity and despair. He sought to put God first amid his tragic circumstances and prove God. The major lesson that we should draw from his life, however, is the importance of a network of friends. Single people, if not more so than their married counterparts, need friendships to balance their lives, and friends with whom to share the experiences and traditions which give life stability and security.

Daniel and his friends may well have been cast together by the adverse circumstances (1:6, 7) of their mutual capture. They soon found that of the vast number carried captive, they shared convictions about spiritual things (1:11-13). Beware of close intimate friendships with those who do not share spiritual interest and exercise. There seemed to be a total absence of jealousy among them (1:17). Instead there was mutual consideration and appreciation (2:49). Daniel had those to whom he could turn for help in a crisis (1:17, 18).

It is of interest that each, however, had to pass through some trials alone. The three Hebrew servants entered the fiery furnace without Daniel (ch. 3). Daniel spent a night amongst lions without them (ch. 6). The lesson here is not so obvious, though none the less present. Don't demand that your friends be identical to you in every way and in every trial. God causes His own to pass through individual circumstances known only to themselves.

These four transplanted Hebrew youths did not sit back and bemoan their circumstances. Doubtless none of them would have chosen the kind of life to which they were called. They did however use the circumstances to the best of their ability. Another has characterized them as those who lived by the principle of the Wise Preacher, "Whatsoever thine hand findeth to do, do it with thy might" (Eccl. 9:10).

The relationship of David and Jonathan illustrates other valuable principles of friendship between single persons. David and Jonathan may well have been teenagers when their friendship began. Their mutual love made no demands upon each other, but freely gave. David did not use his friendship to manipulate Jonathan in any way. There was total unconditional acceptance of each other. Their only concern was for each other's honor (1 Sam. 20:34; 2 Sam. 1:18-27). Encouragement in time of need (23:16-18), appreciation of another's circumstances (2 Sam. 1:18-27), and confiding and confidence (19:2) marked their friendship.

Unmarried Christians must cultivate friendship, investing far more into a relationship than they perhaps are receiving. They must be willing to compromise their demands and self centered interests, avoid manipulation and the use of guilt or pity. These friendships are essential for the emotional well being and spiritual balance of single believers.

It is imperative that mature saints understand, help and encourage those who are single. This embraces treating them as normal, ordinary Christians, not as objects of pity or suspicion.

Single individuals also may need to alter their view of themselves. As another single Christian woman has written "Singleness may or may not be a choice; but joy and contentment are choices, not consequences or circumstances." Remember that your life is of the utmost importance and value to God. You are of value to Him. Consecration and communion, service and success, fulfillment and joy are as available to the single person as to the married.

What has been written is certainly not a total or final answer to the problems and trials which some experience in the single life. It is hoped however that it is the beginning of an answer to the problem confronting many believers.

CHAPTER NINE

Abortion

It was August 9, 1974. The place was the East room of the White House. President Gerald Ford addressed the nation. His speech is remembered for his opening sentence, a sentence which many feel to be his most memorable utterance while in office: "Our long national nightmare is over." President Ford was of course referring to Watergate, the political and legal issue which caused the first resignation in presidential history. While Mr. Ford's words were sincere, he was unaware perhaps that our greatest national nightmare had only begun a few months earlier.

The nineteenth century saw state after state in the United States pass laws to protect the unborn human child. Until 1966, abortion was illegal in every state unless there was clear medical necessity for it. In the twentieth century, abortion began to be more common and accepted in European countries. In the late 60's and early 70's, New York became the first state to liberalize its laws on abortion. Finally on January 22, 1973 the U.S. Supreme Court, in the now infamous Wade versus Roe decision, allowed abortion virtually on demand throughout the first six months of pregnancy, and for medical reasons during the last three. The nightmare had begun and is still continuing.

Each day in the United States, over four thousand

abortions are performed. Each year over 1.5 million pregnancies are interrupted. Abortion has become the second most commonly performed surgical procedure in this country. There is now one abortion for every two live births. Sadly, over 29% are repeat abortion.

Christians feel an innate revulsion at the idea of taking the life of an unborn child. This spiritual instinct is of tremendous value, especially in a day when we face so many issues that seem to have no ready, quick response from the Scriptures. This instinct however must eventually be substantiated with Scripture to prevent it from degenerating into mere foot stomping rhetoric or bias. For those who will patiently persevere with this article, this scriptural basis will be explored.

When an esteemed elder understood that I was attempting an article on this subject, his response was insightful. He commented on the difficulty the subject presents. "You won't find it in Strong's, Young's or Cruden's," he said. And indeed you won't. The reason for this is perhaps so obvious that we lose sight of it and fail to appreciate one of the strongest arguments which Scripture gives. The great lament of the Old Testament was concerning barrenness, not pregnancy. Children were viewed as the heritage of the Lord (Psa. 127:3); the fruit of the womb being His reward and a sign of blessing. No Old Testament saint ever contemplated abortion. Rachel threatened death to herself if she did not have children (Gen. 30:1). "Be fruitful and multiply" was God's intention and desire from Eden onward (Gen. 1:28).

Before we look at some of the Scriptures which have a more direct bearing upon the subject, we should examine carefully the philosophy which has spawned and legitimized this modern means of birth control.

Only eighteen years ago, I stood with over a hundred classmates and recited the Hippocratic oath. That oath contained a promise to never interfere with a pregnancy. Those who were guilty of this were looked down upon by their peers in the medical profession and dealt with severely by both law and medical society groups. So heinous was this crime, only a few short years ago, that its perpetrators were spoken of in the most disdainful tones by colleagues. What has brought about a full 360 degree shift in the winds of opinion? How has the most odious become the most accepted in only 15 years?

No one single reason could begin to answer this question with all its complexity. There are however two very obvious philosophies which controlled the thinking of men through the late sixties and seventies which have influenced to a large extent the current thinking of the masses. I realize that they are not necessarily currently in vogue among front line thinkers, but their effects are still controlling the minds of the masses of men a decade later.

The first of these philosophies was that which sired the "Me" generation. It was the acceptability of looking out for self, for Number One. The law of the jungle returned to civilization and every man had to look out for himself. The end result of this thought process was that everyone had a "right" to do what was best for himself.

Coupled with this was the attempt to dissociate consequences from actions; to somehow divorce forever the need to worry that every action brought inevitable results. Science, technology, money, or at worst your contacts in high places, could take care of the results. God's inviolable law of sowing and reaping was disregarded.

These two lines of thought are by no means new, having had their debut in Eden. The present day, however, saw them refined and made acceptable to men without embarrassment.

The marriage of those two lines of thought led to a new way to look at pregnancy. No longer was it simply a matter of accepting a pregnancy. Now one had a "right" to decide if it was appropriate at this point in time to have a child. If the child were inconvenient, or its birth would interfere with a career, it was perfectly justifiable to "terminate" pregnancy. Thus began the rhetoric of the unwanted child, the right to control one's body, and a myriad of other euphemisms which were created to replace the patent attitude of selfishness and irresponsibility.

We shall look at the shallowness of some of these expressions in the article. Allow me just now to simply underline the fact that if there were no other clearer scriptural reasons to condemn abortion, and there are, the unscriptural attitudes that have fostered the acceptance of abortion would serve to alert us that this is the work of depraved minds and self centered thinking.

But what of the Scriptures? What light do they

shed in a more direct way upon this subject? Any article which touches upon abortion must confront the oft referred to verses in Exodus 21:22-25. This has been appealed to by many in an attempt to show that the unborn child is less than human. Let's look at the verse in its context together:

"If a man strive and hurt a woman with child so that her fruit depart from her, and yet no mischief follow; he shall be surely punished according as the woman's husband will lay upon him... If any mischief follow then thou shalt give life for life."

Now there are several ways of looking at this verse. Scholars differ on its exact meaning as we shall see. They do not however differ on the moral lesson it contains. Some who follow the translation of Spurrell and others translate the expression that "her fruit depart," to mean a premature birth that is able to live, "yet no mischief follow." Thus the death penalty is not exacted because no life was lost. Other scholars, equally competent in the Hebrew language, feel that it does mean that she loses her pregnancy, while she herself is not injured. Some seize on this and build a case upon the difference in value of the unborn child's life and the mother's. They then argue back that since the death of the child was compensated by money and the death of the mother only by a life, that the child is "worth" less than the mother and is somehow less "human" than the mother. The death blow to this reasoning is the context of the chapter. The entire principle of the chapter is one of responsibility and intent, not of relative values from lives. In verse 12, if a man killed another man inadvertently, his life was not immediately forfeit. He was allowed to escape to the city of refuge. In verse 28, if a man's ox were to gore to death by accident another man or woman, the man was not to die but to kill his ox. Was God equating the ox with a man in value? If the owner knew however that the ox was "wont to push with his horn" and did not restrain him, then the ox and the owner were put to death to compensate for the crime. In verse 32, if the ox were to gore a slave, the owner was to pay 30 shekels of silver and the ox was to be stoned. In all of these examples there is no intention on God's part to place relative values on the lives of slaves, men, women, or premature children. It is matter of intention, premeditation and motive.

Come now to Psalm 139. Before we rush headlong into the verses which are of primary concern to us, take a look at the Psalm in its entirety. Its purpose is to detail for us the greatness of God. His attributes are put on display for us to marvel at in adoring worship. The first six verses tell us of His omniscience; the next six show His omnipresence; and as expected, the next four tell us of His omnipotence. It is remarkable however that when the Spirit of God desires to give us an example of the power of God, He does not move to the majesty and greatness of the infinitude of creation. He rather takes us to the tiny developing fetus and the wonder of the creation of a life.

What can we learn from Psalm 139:13-16? One glaring truth is obvious after even a cursory reading of the Psalm. Personhood is established in the womb. The Psalmist refers to God's interest in him, his substance or bones, his unformed substances or embryo (v. 16). God counted him as a person even then. There was identity there; there was personhood with all its value there in the womb. One of the great cries of the pro-choice movement is that every child should be a "wanted" child. Thus if you do not want this baby, don't have him. Think this through for just a moment. This roots the value of one human being in the desires of another. The embryo only has value if I decide it should live. This really reduces the child to not only subhuman value, but inhuman value. Traditionally, we want things and love people. But now we are told that it is up to the mother whether she wants this child to be born; she can decide if it has value. Obviously a very profound shift has occurred in the attitude of society towards all that are unwanted, imperfect and inconvenient to have. It is only a matter of time before the value of every living thing will be determined by another.

The Psalm before us makes clear that God views even the unformed substance, the embryo in its early developmental stages with identity and personhood.

At times our disappointments in searching the Scriptures are of more value than finding what we expect. I looked at the words which Luke the physician uses in his gospel account, when writing in the first few chapters, fully expecting that different words would be used for the unborn children carried by Mary and Elizabeth. To my surprise he used the same word for the fetus, the small infant, even the young child, *brephos*. Not knowing quite what to do with this, since it didn't fit into my idea (I had hoped that Luke would use a special word that would show the fetus was a person), I placed it into the dormant file and did nothing with it. But the obvious fact is so glaring that it begs for display. Luke used the same word for all of these stages of life because each was "brephos." There was no distinction in the amount of humanity which each possessed. Dr. Luke, the medically astute writer, made no distinction in his choice of words between the unborn and born child.

At conception, a complete genetic unit has been formed. Nothing will ever be added to make the embryo more human or a person. Time and size will be added, but not the essence of life.

Psalm 139 also depicts for us God's interest in the prenatal development of the embryo. Some may think this simply poetic language, hyperbole that flows freely from the pen of this writer in the poetic books. May I remind my readers that the Lord Jesus revealed to us that the Father has an interest in the death of every sparrow. How much more appropriate that He has an interest in the birth of every child. In Psalm 139:16, the writer shows God's interest in the development of the fetus from conception to birth. In verses 17, 18, that interest extends even to death and beyond. Remember that the Psalmist is first of all celebrating the greatness and the glory of God; this is not a poetic psalm of the beauty of life. He is telling us about God primarily.

If God has such an intimate interest in the developing fetus, how tragic that those who favour and advocate abortion view it simply as "products of conception," a "non-person" and other such terms. Self interest has replaced and transcended God's interest in the child. We are told that every woman has the right to control what happens to her own body. That is scarcely true even in the other matters of life. Laws frequently regulate what we are allowed to do with our bodies. But putting this point aside for a moment, consider the following. An unborn child is a person with a body. The child has an equal right to control his body or at the very least to have its right protected. The only way around this is to somehow ascribe something less than personhood to the child. This is what abortionists have done.

Far from being an expression of control, abortion is frequently the action taken by a body that was out of control. The activity which led to the pregnancy is where choice is involved. Beyond that, consequences must be expected and accepted.

The unborn child not only possesses an identity and is the object of God's interest, it also displays God's intelligence. The expressions in verses 14, 15 show this, "fearfully and awesome, curiously wrought." The development of the human body is one of God's masterpieces.

But there are several other issues which must be addressed in an article of this nature. A question which is frequently asked, and which the Supreme Court supposedly refused to answer, is "When does life begin?" "When does the soul enter the body?"

Most people are surprised at the early physical development of the fetus. Heart function begins just 14-18 days after conception; at the end of the first month every organ has begun to form; movement of the arms and legs starts at six weeks; brain wave activity can be detected at 43 days. We now include in our definition of brain death the absence of brain waves. Their presence is detectable after only a month and a half of life.

Theologians and church fathers have grappled long over the issue of ensoulment. Some of the earliest ideas included the concept that it was at day 40 for males, and day 80 for females, which was very strange conjecture.

When all the arguments have been weighed, there is one basic question that is left: If it does not happen at conception, then when? Does Scripture help us here?

Consider the unique case of the incarnation of Christ. Every believer would agree that it was Christ in the womb of Mary. His soul was there already. Some may say that this is a unique case. Granted! What of John the Baptist? Was the babe leaping in her womb mere coincidence? If some think this far fetched, be advised that there is a considerable body of evidence bearing upon the subject of intrauterine thought and activity.

Notice also the expression in Psalm 51:5 "In sin did my mother conceive me." If the sinful Adamic nature was there at conception, can any argue that the soul was present? We have nothing in our Bibles to suggest that God gives each man a soul at some moment near birth. Only once in our Bibles does it say that God gave anyone a soul: "God breathed into his nostrils the breath of life, and man became a living soul" (Gen. 2:7). It is the suggestion of this writer that soul is transmitted at conception.

Another aspect that must be faced, and faced with difficulty, is the pregnancy that is the result of crime, completely against the will of the victim. We must first understand that we can never argue from the exception back to the general practice. This today represents a percentage point of a percent of all the abortions performed in this country, but we must face the issue fairly. When a violent act has led to pregnancy, there is one victim; when this is ended by abortion there are now two victims. Doing away with the result of the crime does not lessen the crime or its evil; it does not begin to reverse the trauma done to the woman. We simply add another trauma to her life.

Sin does not lead itself to easy answers. Every sin, every evil deed only brings sorrow in its wake. The options which it opens always are a choice between the lesser of evils. Abortion being a great evil never can answer the problem righteously.

CHAPTER TEN

Solomon's Cure

It is axiomatic that every society values discipline. Its philosophy and form may vary from culture to culture, but its importance is never questioned. Even though we face a crisis in authority in modern western nations today, with an almost schizophrenic mentality, we extol the virtues of discipline. Think only of the high estimation people place upon "well-disciplined" drill teams; think of the effort expended to train "well disciplined" soldiers and commandos! A resumé, or letter of introduction, describing the possessor as having a well disciplined mind or life style is an admirable trait to possess.

From where then does this ability to self discipline arise? Is it a natural trait that only needs proper cultivation? Is it something which is acquired through the experience of life?

In the post war years in America, there arose a new philosophy on discipline. It was a reaction against the harsh, unjustified repression of children. It extolled the virtues of allowing children free expression, and it encouraged permissiveness. Though this vogue has passed from the minds and teaching of many leading psychologists, the effect of this teaching still lingers in the minds and homes of many. This itself underlines two great dangers which we as parents must avoid. There is first of all the danger of creating a false set of alternatives. It is frequently shown how that repressive and excessive discipline is wrong. Many conclude then that the only other alternative is permissiveness. This is a false set of extremes. The Word of God balances us and affords the right approach to discipline.

Carried to their respective extremes, both permissive and restrictive discipline can lead to problems. It is the thesis of this paper that there is a biblical alternative which is known as "authoritative," in which parents enforce standards but also encourage individuality, expression and independence.

The second danger relates to imbibing the thinking of men when it runs contrary to the Bible. Many intelligent, unsaved men, unknowingly endorse the principles of discipline as seen in Scripture. When they do, we can agree with them. When they differ, however, we must in confidence abide by the teaching of God. The very fact that opinions and ideas change from generation to generation should warn against a wholesale acceptance of every new insight that is published.

Much of the harmful teaching that is given is based upon a very wrong supposition. This supposition is that man is basically good and only needs encouragement to nurture his goodness. When children grow up and display traits that are wrong, a frantic search is carried out, looking for "what went wrong." The mentality prevalent is that something has influenced or restricted the child, forbidding his goodness to surface. No Christian needs to be reminded that the plain teaching of God's Word is contrary to this. Psalm 51:5 and

Isaiah 64:6 underscore the inherent problems of the human condition. Paul's New Testament unfolding of the doctrine of depravity is in complete accord with this. While man is capable of doing morally right deeds (witness of Cornelius, Acts 10), his natural tendency is to evil, and he is utterly devoid of any ability to meet his need before God.

There is perhaps no book in our Bible so devoted to the principles of discipline as Proverbs. Its value to us is heightened by the fact that it is a book addressed by a father to his son (1:8). Throughout the book we are presented with contrasts. One of the most common is the wise man and the foolish man. The distinguishing feature in many cases is the ability of the wise man to foresee the consequences of his course, while the foolish pass on blindly. This sense of responsibility is invaluable to ingrain in our children. The awareness of a moral universe with cause and effect, sowing and reaping, action and reaction is one of the chief goals for which parents strive.

These valuable traits are the fruit of discipline in the home. If we follow Solomon's use of the "rod" through Proverbs, we will learn

The Necessity of Discipline.

We have already touched upon this point earlier. Solomon's perspective however should also be heard. Some may think that his mention of the rod carries with it only the idea of corporal punishment. It is enlightening to notice that the Hebrew word for "rod" is actually the same word used in our O.T.

for tribe, scepter, and authority. Its first usage is in Genesis 49:10. Taken together then, it appears that the word carries the thought of the establishment of authority and standards. Bring this thought then down into Solomon's teaching.

In Proverbs 22:15, "Foolishness is bound in the heart of a child, but the rod of correction shall drive it far from him." What Solomon is teaching here (and we shall return to pick up another thread later) is that there is something that is ingrained in the nature of man that needs an external authority to control it. Now it is essential to understand what Solomon is talking about here. "Foolishness" is not a sense of humour or simply a tendency toward lightness. The word in the original contains the idea of stubborness, self will, and refusal. It is rebellion and disobedience that is in view here, not humour or boyishness.

The natural tendency for self will and rebellion must be curbed early. It is often pointed out that Solomon's teaching is balanced by Paul's when he admonished fathers, "Provoke not your children to anger, lest they be discouraged" (Col. 3:21). The danger to be avoided here, according to Paul, is the possibility that a child might not only have a broken will, but a broken spirit. A father who is overly rigid with severe rules and regulations and harsh punishments, who knows only criticism and little, if any, praise, who is quick to note wrong in others but slow to own his own error, is not carrying out Paul's or Solomon's counsel. This leads to a broken and defeated child. Linked with this is the thought expressed in Proverbs 23:14, "Thou shalt beat him with a rod and shall deliver his soul from hell." It is essential that every child learn to recognize and bow to authority. The first place that every child learns this is in the home. One of the goals of home teaching of authority is to prepare the child to recognize God's authority in the moral-spiritual realm. That appears to be the link which Solomon is drawing in his proverb.

It is surprising to hear the thinking of parents in our society today. Many, at times, question me about discipline and its role in the home. They question if they should discipline for fear of repressing some "creative" instinct or destroying the "spirit" of the child. I frequently have to point out how that for the remainder of that child's life he will have to bow to authority in one sphere or another. The signals of the policeman controlling traffic must be obeyed solely because of the authority which his uniform affords him. Yearly taxes must be paid because of the authority of the government. Jobs and careers all involve some order of authority and subordination. If a child does not learn discipline in the home, where will he learn it?

But given that discipline is essential in the Christian home, what of its nature?

The Nature of Discipline

How is a father to carry out his divinely imposed responsibility to establish an atmosphere of authority in the home? Is it accomplished by donning a policeman's uniform, complete with club? Does he become a one man detective agency for the "good of his family?" Does he assume the role of a despot whose word cannot be challenged or questioned?

Insight may be afforded by straying from Solomon one generation. Sadly, Solomon's family did not learn well the lessons which their father taught. Rehoboam was confronted by a crisis in authority when he came to the throne (1 Kings 12). The question which he faced then, which we are considering here, is similar—how to establish authority. The advice of his younger counselors was to threaten his subjects into submission by a show of authority. The older, wiser advisors counselled him to establish authority by serving his people and showing understanding. The results of his ill founded decision are known to all.

An invaluable lesson to underline here is that no one, apart from God, can establish his own authority. I am always a "man under authority." The only way in which a father can have authority is to be the father the Word of God instructs him to be. Coming short, or extending beyond the Scriptures in his parental role will lessen his authority. My authority then is derived from God and His Word. It is incumbent upon me then to know what the Word of God instructs as to parenting.

A mother's authority is also derived from her position as a help-meet to her husband. She gains, not loses authority, by her subjection to his leadership. Friction between parents quickly leads to a breakdown in this chain of authority. Children may begin by trying to listen to both parents, but quickly learn to listen to neither.

I learn then from Solomon and Rehoboam that authority can be established with understanding, patience and love. I am not promoting permissiveness here. The Word of God is affording us an insight into the nature of authority in the home. Consider for just a moment your own case. Why do you bow to the authority of God and His Word? Is it solely because all power is in His hand and discipline will follow if you disobey? Isn't it more because you trust the hand and heart that wields that authority? Do you not bow because you know He loves you and only wants your best?

If our children obey only because of punishment, they may well be obedient children, but they will not be mature. That type of obedience is the lowest rung on the ladder of development. We all strive for willing obedience from our children because they trust and love us, knowing that we are wiser and desire only their good.

Return now to Solomon and his proverbs. In Proverbs 13:24, we read, "He that spareth his rod hateth his son: but he that loveth him chasteneth him betimes." Now we tend to turn this verse around and think that we prove our love to our children when we discipline. The verse however is teaching that love is the basis for the discipline. Because we love, we discipline. Correction, then, is not done in the spirit of anger or revenge. Any parent who disciplines in a rage of anger would be better controlling his own spirit first, before he tries to control another's.

Anger at sin and rebellion is not wrong in itself.

The key is to "be angry and sin not." If you are able to express your anger at the deed without berating the person, then swift and angry judgment will be effective. If, however, you cannot control your anger, then it may be dangerous.

Along with suggesting the motive for discipline, this verse also touches upon the manner. "Betimes" carries the thought of consistency and timeliness. Discipline is hard work. Just ask any parent. Today's rules are enforced, only to be challenged again tomorrow. Allow a child to go beyond limits today and they will automatically assume that liberty from thenceforth. As parents we must assure that our word means exactly what it says. We have all heard parents issue a warning to their children two or three times before finally saying, "Now I really mean it. If you don't do what I say..." What message have they sent to their children? Didn't their word mean it the first time? This is where consistency is so important. Words and warnings must mean exactly what we say or we have weakened our authority before our children.

Discipline is not only hard work, it is a full time job. I am not faulting mothers who must work because of unusual circumstances, but we must never leave the raising of our children to others. To know your child, being sensitive to his personality needs, would appear to me to take all a mother's time and talent. Being a mother at home demands more wisdom than being a career woman in the working world; it is more challenging than the board room; yet it is also more rewarding than the financial benefits of the world.

But discipline must not only be consistent, it should also be swift. This is also embodied in the word "betimes." "Sentence against an evil work" must be carried out speedily (Eccl. 8:11). Threats and warnings of the future mean little to a child.

Discipline should be prompt

Solomon also touches on the methods of discipline. The allusion to the rod itself is valuable. It obviously suggests not only the establishing of authority as we have mentioned earlier, but it embraces the idea of corporal punishment. There is nothing wrong with this form of correction. It is quick and to the point. It is however not the only means of correction. Proverbs 29:15 links it with reproof. At times this may be all that is necessary. If physical punishment is called for, we must remember to display our displeasure at the deed, not our anger at the person. In Proverbs 22:15, to which we have referred, it is rebellion and stubbornness that must be punished, not failure, errors and mistakes.

There must be unity in the setting of standards and in the carrying out of discipline. If there are disagreements, it is far better to voice them in private. Nothing will so undermine the authority and discipline of the home as division between parents. Far better for parents to compromise between themselves and then present a united front, than for each parent to hold out for his or her own style of discipline. Don't allow child raising to divide you as parents. Parenting was never intended to be a popularity contest. It is not your responsibility to make your children love you. Your task is to bring them up in the nurture (training and discipline by example and actions) and admonition of the Lord (Eph. (6:4).

Keep rules to a minimum. Someone has well said "Many rules, many transgressions." Make the rules reasonable. Be fair and willing to discuss from the Scriptures the "why" for your rules. Remember that within the realm of restraint there is independence. The "bit and bridle" which control the horse without understanding (Psalm 32:9) must be slackened to allow the horse to be useful. As children grow in understanding, the reins must be loosened in keeping with their level of maturity.

Neglect of Discipline

In Proverbs 29:15 and 23:13, two results of an undisciplined life are presented. The first involves shame and sorrow in this life: "A child left to himself bringeth his mother to shame." The latter Scripture involves the eternal welfare of the child: "Thou shalt beat him with the rod and shalt deliver his soul from hell."

None of us would advocate the abandonment of discipline. What we do need, however, is to learn in the presence of God and from His Word what constitutes scriptural discipline for the family, and then seek divine help to carry it out in our homes.

CHAPTER ELEVEN

Failing Fathers

In His infinite wisdom, God has provided roles and spheres of responsibility for us all. The potential good of each role is directly proportional to the potential evil that can arise from its abuse. The greater the inherent good, the greater the evil that may arise from failing in that sphere.

Fatherhood is one such sphere ordained of God. It may sadly be true that modern society has traded in parents for baby sitters and day care centers, but God's order remains. In his epistle to the Ephesians, Paul suggests that all fatherhood evolves from God. This should not surprise us. One reason God instituted marriage was to portray the union of Christ and the Church. Family life itself contains and affords tremendous insights into life in the divine family. It came then as no new innovation when God established human fathers with authority and responsibility similar to His own. For those who go in for being a "scriptural" father, the reward is a deepening insight into the Father's heart. Their great joy is to be able to prepare their children to understand God's Fatherhood, when they are converted. For those fathers who choose not to pattern themselves after God's standard, the results are otherwise.

We must be clear, however, that we are not speaking of perfection, but an exercise to approximate as closely as possible the standard of our Bible.

In the historical books of our Old Testament, the Spirit of God has chronicled the family lives of a number of men. In these illustrations, we can view for ourselves the tragedy that results from fathers who failed. The writer finds no great joy in dwelling on the negative; he does not have a secret delight in pointing to the failures of men such as David and Samuel. The examples are here, however, and so placed by the Spirit of God for our learning.

The great emphasis which the Spirit of God has placed upon the role of fathers, underlines a principle which needs to be stressed at the outset, if this article is to be of lasting value to us. God has placed the ultimate burden and responsibility for the welfare of the family upon fathers. Too often we find it convenient to place blame upon our spouses for problems which arise. As the final source of authority in the family, the father is ultimately responsible for the course which is charted, decisions which are made, and the character of discipline administered. This is always done in conjunction with the wife, but the father cannot escape responsibility here.

Notice then with me a few of the fathers whose careers are detailed in Ruth and 1 and 2 Samuel.

Elimelech—The Legacy of a Bad Example

The very first father who engages our attention is Elimelech. Little thought of and even less spoken about, his is the very first name which meets the reader of the delightful book of Ruth. It is not for us now to seek to discover motives or to discern the measure of blame shared by Elimelech and Naomi. His motives may well have been better than we would allow; his degree of culpability perhaps less than we have assigned him, but that has not been opened to us by the Spirit. Without straying from the plain and brief information which we are given, several very important points emerge. It was a day when the judges ruled (v. 1), and moral, spiritual and domestic relationships were so low as to be almost nonexistent. Every man did what he felt to be right; absolutes and standards were as old fashioned as Moses. Here was a man, then, who simply went with the tide.

It is also clear that in a time of trial, he abandoned principles and adopted expediencies. Moab was where food and prosperity were to be had; unseen were the three graves and broken lives that it also harbored.

Upon Elimelech's death, Naomi is left with two sons. Will principle finally prevail? Will the voice of God be heard in the unforseen tragedy? Will Moab's fields be forsaken for the God of Israel's fellowship?

Enter the principle of example. Elimelech had traded principle for profit, now his two sons do the same. Some may object that it was only natural. So it was! Others might argue for the two sons that it was expedient in light of circumstances. So it was! They had learned well from their father.

What type of example are we setting for our children? The long life of faith of Moses was initiated by parents with faith (Heb. 11:23). The principled and devoted life of an Elkanah doubtless had a bearing on Samuel, although we usually stress Hannah's influence. We are teaching our children by word and also by our responses to the problems and trials of life.

Eli—Laxity and Its Fruit

The disastrous story of Eli springs to mind whenever the subject of failing fathers is discussed. While it is difficult to capsulize the failure of Eli into one charge, it would appear that in light of the man of God's denunciation (ch. 2), Eli's failure lay in not carrying out the Word of God in his own family. He was accused of "honoring" his sons before God, of not "restraining" his sons. As high priest, he was responsible to maintain the moral purity of the nation, not to speak of his own family. With moral weakness and with almost apologetic tones he rebuked his sons for their sin and immorality, but this was not enough. God expected Eli to honor Him above his sons in carrying out discipline and maintaining divine standards.

We are by nature creatures of extreme. That is one of our great liabilities. We tend to be either remiss or rough, lax or severe. To walk a balanced path takes constant grace and help from the Lord. It is much easier to discuss and even support the Word of God in the assembly than to carry out those truths day by day in the home. Often Eli-like, we condemn others and their families while excusing our own.

Samuel—Lapse in Consistency

Samuel ranks as one of the greatest men in our Old Testament. He could stand before the nation, in 1 Samuel 12, and challenge any to find evil in him from his "childhood unto this day." Yet when the nation was looking for an excuse to justify asking for a king, they came and pointed to his family. We are informed in 1 Samuel 8 that when he was old he made his two sons judges in Beersheba. Unlike their father, they were marked by evil. It may well be that their moral bankruptcy in no way reflected Samuel's parenting. Yet here were men who had been placed in positions of responsibility, failing to live godly lives.

It could well be pointed out that their sphere of influence was rather small, being only Beersheba, and that the indignation of the people was hypocritical. All this is granted. Yet the issue remains that Samuel had perpetuated Eli's error on a much smaller scale. He had shown favoritism to his sons.

What was in reality a very small inconsistency in Samuel's life afforded an excuse for the people to clamor for a king. God knew their hearts and brushed aside their pretense in His condemnation of the nation.

Consistency in family life is imperative. This includes not only matters of discipline, but also personal living and our spiritual lives. Our children are quick to detect inconsistency in our behavior. This may then be used to excuse blatantly wrong actions on their part.

Jesse—Lack of Confidence

When Samuel came to anoint a king from amongst Jesse's sons, he assembled Jesse and his sons together. This aged patriarch called together seven of his eight sons. He failed to call David. Was this mere oversight? It would appear that Jesse committed an error all too frequent even today. He lacked confidence in David for the office which Samuel was seeking to fill. He judged simply by what was natural: age, stature, size, rank. He failed to appreciate what God saw in David.

Being the youngest, David was set aside and perhaps considered unimportant to the family and its fortunes. To David's credit, he never displayed any bitterness or hostility towards his family despite provocation (1 Sam. 17:28). Other children however have not been so fortunate. At times a parent will favor one child over another because of some natural ability or personal resemblance. Recall to mind the divided family of Isaac and Rebekah, with each favoring one of the children. Favoritism and partiality may engender anger and frustration. To be overlooked, snubbed, denied, and perhaps degraded because of a lack of physical or intellectual talents may prove difficult to accept. We may think this very foreign from our ways, but a moment's reflection may reveal that we are very prone to this. The boy who does not have his father's physical prowess, the girl who lacks her mother's talents, the child who does not follow in a parent's footsteps intellectually, may feel as though they have disappointed their parents. As parents we must strive to impart to our children an atmosphere of unconditional love; love which is not dependent upon accomplishments but only upon relationship.

Saul—Liability of Willfulness

All these imperfections in the rearing of our children are really only manifestations and fruit of our fallen natures. It is not surprising, then, that the person who typifies the flesh with all its inherent evil should also display for us many of the most undesirable qualities for parents. Saul was an absolute disaster as a father. His errors were in several critical spheres. The result of it all was that he literally destroyed his family so that David had to inquire and search if there were any left of the house of Saul.

It is startling that the man who treated God's word so lightly in 1 Samuel 13, is ready to put his own son to death only one chapter later because he unknowingly disobeyed his orders. Rather than this being a case of unsparing discipline, it reveals the tendency of Saul to abuse his own family for his own interests. We notice also that he used his children for his own selfish ends. His daughters are used in an attempt to ensnare David (1 Sam. 18); Jonathan is expected to betray David (ch. 19), and he cursed and shamed his own children for not conspiring with him (20:30-34). He used Michal almost as a trinket to lure and then punish David (1 Sam. 24:44). There is no thought of the happiness or will of God for his children. It is reduced simply to whether or not his children fulfill his will and live for advancing his purposes.

This may seem like very strong language, and no doubt it is. But is there not, however, a principle here with which we can identify? Is there not a tendency for us as parents to also approve or disapprove of our children on the basis of our will rather than God's? Is it that far fetched to think that some parents use their children to live out their own fantasies and desires? Who among us has not checked himself and had to confess to God the sin of seeking to push our children to do what we always wanted to do?

Whatever my personal desires for my children, be they materialistic, such as place or prestige in this world, or be they spiritual such as desiring a missionary or evangelist, if they are not the will of God, they are wrong. Worse yet, however, is to withhold approval or acceptance because a child does not follow my desires.

In his dealings with family, friends, associates and even whole cities such as the Ziphites, Saul displayed two additional and interrelated traits, the use of guilt to manipulate, and the use of self pity. He sought to achieve his ends by instilling in others a sense of his misfortune and of their obligation to feel sympathy and pity for his plight. Nothing was too low to use as a means to this end.

Many parents think that the primary goal before them is to get their children to obey. Some unconsciously employ guilt to manipulate and control. This may achieve the desired goal of a sort of "obedience" which is really compliance. But it falls far short of what a father's goal should really be. Autocratic rule and subservience are not the ideal for which to strive. My primary responsibility, from the Scriptures, is to display traits of fatherhood that will enlighten my family as to the character of God. His great objective is to control by love and loyalty borne of confidence and trust. Constraining my children through a sense of guilt may well achieve obedience, but it will not achieve "the nurture and admonition of the Lord."

Saul sought to live his life through his children. He attempted to control the lives of his children for his selfish ends. He endeavored to use his children to punish others. He succeeded in consigning one daughter to barrenness (2 Sam. 6:23), in leaving three sons slain upon Mount Gilboa (1 Sam. 31), and sentencing seven grandsons to death at the hands of the Gibeonites (2 Sam. 21). His own life ended in shame, ignominy, and suicide.

The lessons which issue from such a life are sober and searching. There are no Sauls amongst us for which we thank God. There may, however, be a little Saul in each of our hearts. It must be the will of God for our children, their happiness and usefulness, their blessing, and not our own relived lives and desires that matter. We must take the time to become students of our children, assessing their needs emotionally and spiritually, and not simply putting them into some ready made mold. All children are unique, different, possessing their own potential and talents. It is our responsibility and privilege to discover and nurture these. Far better to be like Elkannah and Hannah and yield our

Samuels to the will of God, than like Saul to raise barren Michals whose lives end in despair.

David—Lessons That Humble

David had the tragic experience of burying four sons. His grievous sin with Bathsheba was the starting point that led to four funeral corteges. Prior to his sin, David shed many tears which God put into His bottle (Psa. 56:8). After his fall, it was not God who did the counting of his tears, but David. Tears flowed freely again, not now because of the hardness and sin of others, but because of his own sin.

David not only saw four sons taken from him, but had the humbling experience of seeing his own sins reflected in his children. Perhaps someone reading this may not identify with this. If so, allow me to assure you that the most humbling aspect of parenting, along with our sense of shortcoming, is the viewing of our own failures reproduced in our children. No doubt God intends to teach us about ourselves from this. The lesson nevertheless is humbling. Who has not reigned in his anger, when about to denounce the error of his child, because Nathan's arrow stuck fast in his own conscience, "Thou art the man"? This repetition of weaknesses and inconsistencies is meant to reveal to us our deficiencies, casting us more upon our Father.

David saw his lust and immorality replayed on a larger scale in his son Ammon. His arrogance and murder of Uriah were all reproduced in the infamous career of Absalom. When David wailed

"Would God I had died for thee," it was not merely a desperate wish to have died in Absalom's stead. David in hindsight was longing that God would have taken him away in discipline rather than allowing him to live. Sudden, severe judgement may well have restrained the natures of Ammon and Absalom.

David's sin followed him to his deathbed. As the aged king lies breathing out his last, Adonijah usurps the throne. "His father," we are told, "had not displeased him at any time." We are told that his mother bare him after Absalom. Why was David weak in regard to succession? Was it simply age? Is there not a hint that it was because Adonijah was Absalom's brother? Conscience was still at work. Feeling responsibility for Absalom's tragic end, he may have tended to be lenient with his brother to compensate.

We have seen together the collective errors of some of the great men of God, and some of the not so great. It reminds us forcibly that none of us is exempt from these dangers. As fathers, we are called upon to raise our children in the "nurture and admonition of the Lord," to "provoke not" our children to wrath and anger (Eph. 6:4). These brief, terse injunctions from the Spirit of God, through the pen of Paul, summarize the positive aspect of all the failures at which we have looked. The idea of nurture and admonition carries with it example as well as teaching and discipline. We are not to provoke to wrath because the danger of discouragement (Col. 3:21) is very real. This does not mean that we try to please our children, but rather avoid constant berating, degrading and negative, harsh criticism. Praise and approval are potent agents in promoting change and in reinforcing positive character traits. It will hinder us from Jesse's error of overlooking David and from Saul's manipulating of his children for selfish ends.

Above all, the Word of God would remind us that as imperfect men, we are prone to extremes and excesses, to shortcomings and lapses in our parenting. It will cast us upon God more and more, resulting in the prayer of Manoah being often upon our own lips, "How shall we order the child and how shall we do unto him?" (Judges 13:12).

CHAPTER TWELVE

Parents with Priorities (1)

The wisdom of God has fortunately not left us with only negative examples to avoid, but has also provided positive models from which to learn. Parenting has always been an extremely difficult job. Imagine the grief of the first parents when they became aware that family life could be as deeply tragic as Cain caused it to be.

One of the most distressing aspects of parenting is that most of us receive "on the job" training. Just when we feel that we have learned invaluable lessons and are equipped for the task, we are no longer needed in that role. There we are with a storehouse of wisdom which no one else really wants. Yet this on the job training is obviously what the Lord intended. Raising children was meant to educate us as much as to train them.

Encouragement is provided by noting some of the parents in the Scriptures who left us positive examples to follow. Although direct instructions for parenting are limited, observation of those who "succeeded" in their roles is abundant. Consider those who had the priority of—

Living Before Their Children

Someone else has aptly remarked that "attitudes are caught, not taught." Sociologists and psychologists both agree that the most powerful influence in shaping children is the example to which they are exposed. The mandate for all christian parents is first of all to live before their families in such a way as to commend the truth of God. This does not imply perfection. Like the teacher to whom James refers (James 3:2), in being examples "we offend all." Yet just as the Lord looked at the tenor of a man's life and not his lapses, so we should seek to live consistently before our families.

Consider the opening of II Timothy. This epistle, which is occupied with the continuity of testimony, begins with a short yet eloquent commentary on Timothy's home life. Paul makes reference to Timothy's mother and grandmother, Lois and Eunice. When Paul alludes to the "unfeigned faith" of Timothy, he is not referring simply to that which linked him to Christ, but to the principle of faith by which he lived. He then goes back two generations and, embracing both Lois and Eunice, connotes that faith was first of all real; it was genuine. Timothy had seen it in action in the family. His family environment had consisted of a saved mother and an unconverted father. There were doubtless many opportunities for him to witness the reality of his mother's life of faith. Faith, we are told, dwelt in them. It was at home in their hearts. It was not a Sunday only resident. It was not like the fire alarm box marked "use only in emergency." It was perfectly at home and natural for everything to be consistent with this great principle. Doubtless, the principle of faith reigned in the household. Every problem and decision was subjected to this tenet.

Every perplexity was submitted to this maxim. It is little wonder, then, that their faith was reproduced in Timothy. It was not that God rewarded their life of faith by saving Timothy. That is not the point. Timothy had seen a consistent life lived before him; when converted, this example had a tremendous influence on his way of life.

Early in recorded history, we are introduced to Enoch, of whom it is said that "he walked with God." This is no little accomplishment in itself. Yet the Spirit of God obviously desires to convey something more for He tells us that he walked with God and begat sons and daughters; then the Spirit adds again. "And Enoch walked with God." Family life did not hinder Enoch's walk. He not only walked with God but also walked before his family. This habit of living before God can be traced down to his great grandson, Noah.

Living before our children is vital. Failure to do so on a consistent basis will undermine all the other principles which follow. It must again be emphasized that no suggestion of expertise or faultlessness is being suggested, it is the tenor of one's life that is important.

Another priority with Biblical parents was—

Leading Them.

The divine visitor to the pilgrim tent in the plains of Mamre commended Abraham when He said, "I know him, that he will command his children and his household after him" (Gen. 18:19). The Deuteronomic repetition of the law is punctuated by a divine injunction that parents were to keep these truths before the family. This involved teaching by repetition (Deut. 6:7), as well as making the Word of God an integral part of daily life. It was not a case of piously quoting verses at various times, but of weaving the principles and truths of Scripture into everyday life. The most common of activities would afford opportunity for the Scriptures to be learned and applied. The application of the Scriptures to everyday problems, the balancing of current opinions by divine values, the comparison of behaviour of others against scriptural standards, all "teach" the Scriptures and develop a value standard for our children.

Seasons were set aside when generations yet to come would ask the father of the home concerning the spiritual history of the nation. Instruction in divine truth and ways was to be a part of family life.

It is the responsibility of parents to imbue their children with a value system and to teach them not just what to think, but how to think. All who have raised their families will readily testify to how rapidly the years seem to pass. All too soon that fragile infant is ready to step out into a cynical world. Have we prepared them for the attack upon their character and integrity, as well as we have prepared them for the attack upon their faith? Only by patient application of the Scriptures through all the circumstances of life, the spending of time with our children, the winning of their confidence, can we hope to so prepare them. It is far more important to provide them with the key into your life than with the keys to the car.

God does not hold us responsible for what our children do, but for what we have taught them. The obligation of leadership is awesome. Though we have stressed the spiritual aspect of life, it justly involves every aspect of life for which you are preparing your child: social, intellectual, employment, financial, as well as spiritual. This preparation is a full time task involving both parents, for each have unique and invaluable contributions to make to children. It should not be left to chance or even to others. We have the privilege as well as the obligation to lead our children into increasing spheres of responsibility and preparedness.

Leaving a Legacy

The result of living before our children and leading them as parents will be a rich legacy upon which they can build. No, this is not the legacy that comes from an attorney's office when the will is read. Hopefully, each of us will have the joy of actually seeing this legacy used before our eyes, in our lifetime, if the Lord be not come. This is an intangible legacy, immaterial, yet vastly more valuable than any estate ever bequeathed.

When David stared death in the face and saw a young and tender Solomon about to ascend the throne, he purposed to prepare with all his might for his son (I Chron. 22:5). In this chapter, David prepared Solomon as well as the materials with which Solomon was to build the temple. Foresight and forethought enabled David to prepare for this. Although David's legacy was material, it was not for Solomon's wealth but for God's glory. He left his son a legacy with which to honor God.

Moses' parents left him a legacy of faith. In Hebrews 11, the faith life of Moses is introduced with a reminder that Amram and Jochebed, moved by faith, hid Moses for three months. One can only imagine with what fear they committed their small infant to the care of God as they placed him in the ark and set it by the water's edge. Little wonder that the Spirit of God can follow their encore with the recital of "by faith Moses" four times.

How often would Moses have been told by his mother of those early months and of the faithfulness of God? It is impossible to calculate the immense impact that it must have had, shaping convictions and inspiring confidence in God.

The history of Onesiphorus could be recorded and condensed into two sentences. Yet he has earned for himself a place of eternal honor, and he earned for his family a rich blessing.

Consider the legacy this man left by his conduct. Paul is a prisoner in Rome. It is not a comfortable hired house now, but perhaps a damp, dark hole in the ground into which he has been placed. No special name plate was above his "cell", but thrown in amongst the other criminals of the day, he was lost in that vast prison system of Rome. Friends who once stood with Paul now shun him. The danger and cost are too great. These fair-weather friends were not apostates. Most were probably true believers who failed to come forward to associate themselves with Paul. The "day" shall declare their motives. Paul prayed that it "might not be laid to their charge" (II Tim. 4:16).

Yet amidst this dark scene, Onesiphorus shines for God. The desertion of others only highlights the devotion of Onesiphorus. Undeterred by the opinion of others, the obstacles before him, or his own business obligations in Rome, we read that he sought out, found and refreshed Paul. We see his courage in not being ashamed of Paul; his compassion and care in that he oft refreshed him; his conscientious concern was appreciated by Paul for he remarks that he sought him out very diligently. Paul adds to this terse yet eloquent portrait that Onesiphorus was not simply seeking a place in history by ministering to Paul in distress. This had been his consistent habit even at Ephesus.

Little wonder then that Paul can say "The Lord give mercy unto the house of Onesiphorus." Whether this hero of the faith was alive or with his Lord is not that critical. What must be appreciated is that as a result of his life, blessing was to fall upon his family. We should all covet, David-like, the ability to bless our families (II Sam. 6:20).

Many of us have the privilege of looking back at parents who left us legacies that are invaluable. By contrast, many a family has risen up in fellowship with the brother of Luke 12:13 and demanded more of a material inheritance. Bitter words and irreconcilable feelings have issued from such bequests. Tragic ends and wasted fortunes have not been infrequent. Yet here is a legacy which, like the blessing of the Lord, makes rich and carries no sorrow in its wake. The godly example of a consistent life, the display of character and consistency amidst trial, the adherence to principles even at personal loss, a life lived for God and with God, all produce an estate that cannot be evaluated by earthly standards.

Is leaving such a legacy a priority with us? Do we, as fathers, feel that as long as we have provided the material needs for our families that we have met all our responsibilities? Priorities involve day to day living, not just the major crises of our lives.

There are those who have sacrificed promotion and transfer simply because there was no assembly in the city to which they would have to move. Others have turned down careers in the world to be able to be at home with children and raise them for the Lord. Rare is the person who has ever looked back upon such a legacy with a desire to exchange it for a material one.

In developing a sense of family and closeness, the value of traditions cannot be over emphasized. Our society has sadly linked this concept with materialism in one form or another. It is not however, how much money is spent, but how much time is given, that is important. We must learn to share more than our genetic pool with our children, and to develop more than our physical similarities.

Traditions, be they holidays, birthdays, or special days, make children feel special and significant in their parent's eyes. It brings security, predictability, and structure to a child's life. It creates bonds that cannot be severed. When the bonds of control are loosed at maturity, these are the links which hold families together in a meaningful way. Each family can develop their own traditions and special days. It may be a favorite place to visit, a special holiday or birthdays. What is important is the time spent together and the predictability of the event.

As we live before our children, lead them into spheres of responsibility and moral and spiritual development, we shall be enabled to leave them a rich legacy upon which to build for the future. This is both our privilege and our responsibility as parents before the Lord. Yet the ultimate test is our success in letting go.

CHAPTER THIRTEEN

Parents with Priorities (2)

Letting Go

Perhaps the most difficult task which many of us face is that of letting our children go, granting them their independence. There really are many reasons why this letting go process is so difficult. There is a great stress today placed upon bonding between parents and child. This is one of the strong arguments that has opened up the delivery room at the hospital to the father. Bonding occurs very early and is essential. Yet no one talks about letting go. Parenting is almost unique in that successful parents actually work themselves out of their job. The better parents do at their job, the less children will need them when they are adults. Dependent, clinging children who require their parents for decision making and to rescue them from problems, may gratify their parent's egos and sense of need, but are not functioning well as mature adults.

What is "letting go"? What does it mean? Is it pushing our children out into the world? The word actually denotes the ultimate purpose of parenting: to raise our children to function in the world, seeking God's will for their own lives. It is not a cruelty but a kindness; it is not a mistake but a mandate. It is far reaching and very practical. It does not mean refusal to help or give counsel when it is requested. It does mean however, not seeking to control by demand, interference, or the use of guilt. This embraces our children and their families. It will keep parents and in-laws out of the problems of their children unless invited in. It will respect the autonomy and maturity of those whom we raised. A lack of confidence in them only reveals a lack of confidence in how well we prepared them for adulthood.

Consider the Biblical basis for this: Children are God's gift to us. They are "the heritage" of the Lord (Psa. 127:3). They are loaned to us to raise for God. Each of us should drink deeply of Hannah's spirit. Samuel was not "hers", he belonged to the Lord. She returned him for God to use. Children are not our possessions. We have a stewardship to raise them. Ours is the privilege of being able to critically influence the lives of others for God. With every scriptural stewardship, the emphasis is upon being faithful. When that stewardship is accomplished, we return them to the will of God, not to our wills for their lives. None of us will ever be called upon to rival Abraham in his display of "letting go," yet is there not in his sacrifice of Isaac something of this principle? The dearest object to his heart was given back to God as being more God's than his.

In Deuteronomy 32:10, 11 God's dealings with Israel are chronicled for us. We are told that God "found him...led him...instructed him...kept him..." This could well correspond to what has been discussed under earlier headings. While we might judge God's ways complete as described, He had one final point to teach them. "As an eagle stirreth up her nest, fluttereth over her young, spreadeth abroad her wings, taketh them, beareth them on her wings, so the Lord..." What is the picture? That of the eagle preparing her young for independence. It is not certainly the thought that God desires us to live independent of Himself. Rather God was preparing His people for living in the land, mature and capable of decisions.

God was, with Israel and also with us, continually leading us to more full-grown stature. This never dissolves bonds, but replaces the ties of infancy with a relationship that is far more satisfying and honouring to Him.

When nations grant independence to once former territories or colonies, it is not with the idea of dissolving all bonds, but of maintaining and strengthening what was vital and valuable, while doing away with what is no longer needed.

It is the same with parents. God has given us children for a few short years to raise and then to deliver back to Him that they might live their lives according to His will and for His glory. This is precisely why "letting go" is so difficult.

Bear with me a minute and see if these truths do not find an echo in your heart. After raising a child for eighteen years, we have a tremendous investment in him. We are confronted first of all with the idea of "losing" something. It is naturally against our instincts. Granting them independence is also difficult because our identity is so wrapped up in our children. What they do reflects upon us and we are often afraid. To relinquish control of their lives means just that. We can no longer dictate or influence the choices which they make. Instinctively, some parents begin to tighten the reins that bind them to their children. This only leads to conflict and, at worst, rebellion. At the very stage when development suggests granting further freedom, a tightening of control causes tragic confrontation.

Sadly in some instances, the role of the dependent child has been reversed and now parents become dependent on their children and "need" them. I am not speaking now of physical handicaps or illness, but of an emotional need to control the life of another or to feel "needed" and appreciated. The Lord did not place children into our homes to satisfy our needs. That is a reversal of roles.

Though Paul may not have had any natural children, he displayed remarkable wisdom and grace in the manner in which he raised his spiritual sons. His dealings with Titus and Timothy are cases in point. He gradually gave increasing responsibility with corresponding expressions of approval and confidence. He "raised" sons who would be able to function in his absence.

Recall the prodigal's father in Luke 15 for a most remarkable insight into "letting go." A day came when the son had reached his majority and demanded the right of independence. This act of "letting go" involved a temporary grief with the hope of an eventual greater joy. The father did not choose to dictate right and wrong to his son. That had obviously been his occupation for all the past years. Now that training would be put to the test. His grant of freedom did not cause the father to lose anything, except possibly a few night's sleep. He gained far more in the end from a much more stable and valuable relationship.

The Scriptures do afford us illustrations of those who sought to interfere with their families. Zebedee's wife made her way to the Lord. To her credit it must quickly be added that her intentions were good. It may even be that this was a family plot. With expressions of worship and supplication upon her lips she approached the Lord. Her request was simple: she wished for her two sons to have the distinction of sitting beside the Lord in His coming kingdom. Mary had good intentions, even spiritual desires for her sons. Yet the Lord's rebuke made it evident that even spiritual desires have to be subject to the will of God.

Mary, the mother of the Lord, sought to control her Son. In John 2 she tried to direct His activity, thinking perhaps that it was time for Him to display His inherent power or begin to display His credentials to the nation. At other times, she with her family sought to claim Him and interfere with His service (Mark 3:31-34). In His childhood He was obedient and submissive to His parents (Luke 2:51). As an adult, He honoured His mother (John 19:25-27) but did not allow her to control Him. The will of God for Him as a child was to be subject to His parents. The will of God for Him as an adult was far different than what Mary intended. His obligation was to the will of God, not the will of Mary.

Laban failed to realize that he had given his daughters to Jacob, still feeling that he had some claim upon them (Gen. 31). He pursued after them with the intent of retrieving what he felt to be his

(Gen. 31:26-29). Only the word of God restrained him.

It is clear from the Word of God that we must let go of our children. It is also clear why this must be so. It is far more difficult to actually do it. We should look upon it more as a process than an act. The years which we invest in them are the gradual road toward independence. As more responsibilities are given and accomplished, as confidence increases, and as maturity in thought develops, we simply recognize what already exists: that a mature, independent individual has developed. It is not a matter so much of an age being reached as an attitude and character being evidenced.

I recall trying to teach one of the girls to ride her bike. I held on and ran alongside while she continued to demand that I not let go. Finally the day came when I did let go, but continued to run alongside. A bit later I let go and stopped running. She was on her own. She had learned to make her own way. If she fell and hurt her knee, I was still there. But the bike was in her hands. I had helped and directed all I could. Her course, speed and destination were now up to her.

May the Lord enable us all as parents to establish priorities in our lives which will result in our children entering life with a rich spiritual and moral legacy and the preparedness to live for God and Christ, confident that we desire not control, but the will of God for them.